GIVING A
CHILDREN'S PARTY

GIVING A CHILDREN'S PARTY

Jane Cable-Alexander

with photographs by
Sandra Lousada and John Cook

TREASURE PRESS

Jigsaw cards (see page 71)

To Henrietta

First published in Great Britain in 1980 by
Park Lane Press

Published in 1983 by
Pelham Books Ltd

This edition published in 1988 by
Treasure Press
59 Grosvenor Street
London W1

ISBN 1 85051 263 9

Printed in Hong Kong

CONTENTS

INTRODUCTION

Giving a party for children is one of the most satisfying forms of entertaining. Fierce critics they may be, but they are also highly appreciative, and your careful planning and hard work are well rewarded. Young children haven't acquired the degree of embarrassment that accompanies older children at parties, and original ideas are well worth trying out on them. Going to parties is one of the stages in the progressively developing social skills of a child. Playgroup leaders will tell you all about the different types of small child; the one who is the natural leader, ebullient and enthusiastic, and the shyer, quieter child who is happiest doing his own thing either on his own or with a great friend. You'll recognise the two types at your parties – right from an early age. It is debatable which it is best to have, a collection of noisy children who, whilst they are obviously enjoying themselves, reduce you to shreds by the end of two hours; or a collection of quiet uncommunicative children who, though models of behaviour, make you wonder if it's all worth while. The answer is, of course, that a party is a collection of all types, gathered together for one purpose, and that is to enjoy themselves. And a group of children enjoying themselves doesn't mean that you shouldn't have a good time too, so whilst you are busy supervising them don't forget there's nothing to stop you getting on your hands and knees for the slow tortoise race, or blowing ping-pong balls along the carpet with a straw; and adults love three legged races and sack races. Whilst enjoyment for all is obviously uppermost in your mind, don't be afraid to assert your authority and check rampaging children. After all, it's your child who will suffer the loss if you examine broken china and say 'I'll never have that lot in the house again'. Whereas a firm hand at the right time can save upset.

Parents seem to fall into two main categories, those who enjoy an open house and aren't too bothered by anything, and turn their hand to most things successfully, and those with neater lives who prefer things better organised and to whom spontaneity is almost an unknown word. The first group will probably happily have given successful parties for years for all the family as they have grown up, and the second will dutifully and painfully have given the required birthday party for each child and breathed a sigh of relief when it's all over. It's no good pretending you are one type if you are the other, but the ideas in this book could possibly help the first group to be better organised and prepared, and the second group may glean some ideas that will enable them to be more adventurous and original. A wild generalisation? But perhaps the spontaneous personalities were the noisy extroverts at children's parties and the introverts grew into the Mothers who find it all a bit of an effort.

Although the word 'Mothers' naturally crops up rather frequently in the book, (after all most people who organise children's parties *are* Mothers), this book is for Fathers too. The majority of men are very much part of a family, and any help from them is *always* welcome, but not always very forthcoming. Most men have a dread of children's parties which is a pity, because they can have a devastatingly useful effect on rebellious small boys. Small girls too! Finish up a party with a wrestling match on the floor, Father underneath, being tickled and teased by swarms of children and it's voted the best part of the party! You're lucky of course, if your husband will consent to go this far, but if you can persuade him to come and help with the games or the gramophone – do, he'll probably end up by thoroughly enjoying it all. Nowadays there are more and more Fathers bringing up children on their own, sometimes plunged into it quite unexpectedly, and all the things they never had to think about suddenly have to be dealt with. If this is you, and a full scale party defeats you, and cash is short, don't despair, there are plenty of cheap and original ways to entertain children without giving the conventional party, and some of the things included in the 'Ideas' chapter (see page 29) will help you out. Let nobody forget the bachelor godfather or uncle, who because he's not involved with children the whole time, is often absolutely marvellous value at a children's party, and has an enormous capacity for getting everyone to enjoy themselves.

After all, that's what it's all about – enjoyment, and amidst all the cautionary advice on burns at cooking parties and litter on nature walks, never lose sight of why everyone is there – to enjoy themselves. Parties are essentially social activities; they exist to make new friendships, cement old ones, pay back kindnesses, and give pleasure to children. So if you are new to a district, and your child is new to the school, why not give him or her a party? They will have a chance to ask people they like, and from that may well spring new friendships for you, and in no time at all the strangeness and loneliness of a new area will turn into a feeling of belonging.

This book is aimed at helping you give a successful party. It is full of ideas for organisation, themes for parties, food, games, decorations, and all the little touches that help to make the party a good one. Instead of wishing you had thought of something after the party, here is where to find it all before. Use it as a sounding board, look on it all as a pleasure, get organised, relax, and enjoy yourself. Then you may be sure that everyone else will.

CHAPTER 1

PLANNING AND PREPARATION

You've committed yourself; you've agreed to give a party for your child, or else you've decided to arrange one for them, and the next thing to fix is when and where to have it, how many children to ask, and what to do with them. When you've thought of that, you've then got to decide what games they are going to play and what everyone is going to eat, so all in all it looks a pretty formidable task. Is this because adults have lost the knack of unbending at parties, and mixing easily with a group of children – becoming strangely embarrassed with a crowd of them? It's odd to think it could be this way round, but it *is* a nerve-racking thing giving a party, so the better prepared you are for it the better it will go. Organisation is the key word here. It makes it sound a bit pompous, but the better organised and prepared you are, the more chance there is of the party being a success.

When?

First of all then, when? Birthday parties are, of course, the most popular, but don't forget there are plenty of other times to entertain children. What if your son's birthday is in early February and you have a huge garden ideal for a barbecue party, do you have a conventional indoor party, or explain that if he waits he can have lots of friends to a summer barbecue? And if your daughter's birthday is on a Sunday, do you have the party on an afternoon when a lot of people are either doing something and resent being dragged out to ferry children to and from parties, or wait until the holidays and give one then? Parties in the holidays are enormously appreciated by other parents, especially in the summer holidays when the last few weeks can seem hard to fill, and an invitation to a beach party or a trip up the river can inject new life into everyone. If you haven't a large garden or live in a flat, and can't have children thumping about without fear of annoying neighbours, think along other lines and organise an outing. It doesn't have to be in the summer either; off season winter trips and Christmas exhibitions are good value, and never as crowded as popular summer events. If you have a baby and small children, why not organise a pram-pushing party in the park with some other young mothers in the same street or block of flats? You'll find some ideas on how to amuse the youngsters in the chapter 'Ideas' (see page 29). Perhaps this will spark off some new ideas for you, and a party can become a regular gathering of young mothers with children

of the same age. You may even find yourself with some free afternoons on your hands as a result, as some mothers take it in turns to look after a group of children and others take time off.

Where?

Now you've decided when to have it, you must arrange the place. Of course, for most people, one's own home is the obvious place, but if this is impractical because your home is either too small, or you want to ask more children than you've room for, consider other places. If you live in a village,

A party in one's own home?

the village hall fits the bill beautifully. It's large, often has a piano, and chairs and tables are at the ready. There are lavatories and wash basins for all, and plenty of room to play energetic team games. The Clerk of the Parish Council will tell you if you can hire it for the afternoon, but look ahead and book it well in advance. This applies to anything you've planned to take children to – book ahead and get better seats, entertainers and the like and have the comfortable feeling of knowing everything is organised.

A wise idea is not to tell the children what you plan to do until you have made arrangements, they can be terribly disappointed if their hopes are raised only to be dashed because you have left everything until too late. A word of warning, community rooms can sometimes be freezing in winter, so check on the heating arrangements if you plan to have a winter party in one. Kind friends may lend barns or garages; if you are enterprising and offer to clear them out in return for holding a barn dance or barbecue in them, everyone benefits. You may, of course, be wildly lucky and get hold of a houseboat or something really original, but such chances are rare. A very successful children's party was given in a marquee the evening after a wedding; adults came too, but the children held the little dance floor and helped with the records and everyone enjoyed themselves enormously. It shows what a little enterprise and initiative will do. If you are prepared to go to extra expense think about hiring a room in a local hotel; they say they cater for weddings and parties, and some do good arrangements for children. It is expensive though, and for most people out of the question, so they hold the party in their own home.

How many?

Now you go on to plan how many children to ask, and who to ask, both of which can be the most difficult thing to arrange. For this is the bit that your child will have a major hand in, and even small children will have amazingly tenacious views on this. By dint of clever suggestion you can get them to agree on a time and a place, but try and dictate who is going to come, and you are in deeper water. Sometimes it can appear that short of asking the entire class, you are going to have to scrap the whole thing. Resorting to an outing if you really can't accommodate large numbers of children solves the problem. Say very firmly that they can only take two people, and it's easier than saying they can ask ten or twelve friends from school. Selection can cause endless heartbreak, but be firm; if you can't cope with a large number say so at the beginning, and stick to it. When you have got the time, place and a list of names, send out the invitations. It sounds a surprisingly simple thing to do, but even that can be beset with pitfalls for the inexperienced. Post ten invitations, and you've already put the minimum of a pound on the cost of a party at these days' prices. Hand them to the children to give out at school, and they may not get delivered promptly, or replies get lost. A good way, if you know other Mothers fairly well from waiting outside school for your children, is to hand the invitations to them personally, and then you can get in the request that you would like to know if the children can come. Your child can hand out the rest. Do try and give plenty of notice; most people have pretty busy lives nowadays, and a request on Thursday for a party on Saturday, especially if it is for your child's best friend, doesn't go down too well if he can't come. The best thing to do when drawing up the list is to decide whom in particular is going to be asked, and clearing a date with them first. You probably know the parents well anyway, and a mutual date can be fixed between you. A party isn't a party at six years old without one's best friend. Another point you must decide is the length of time you are going to have it

for. Younger children find one and a half to two hours the most they can take without becoming fractious, and even older children find it hard to sustain interest after three hours. State clearly on the invitation the time of arrival and departure, and then hope everyone turns up on time. For small groups of children who live nearby your best safeguard for getting them away on time is to offer to take them home, and then firmly pile them in the car and deliver them at the appointed hour. Or walk them home, a brisk walk will dispel any feelings of irritation that may have accumulated on your part. Do state what the children should wear, if it's an outdoor party it's best to be on the safe side and stipulate that they bring boots and anoraks to change into if the garden's muddy, as you've no idea what the weather will be like if you send the invitations out two weeks in advance. For a Barn dance (see page 39) for instance, state the order of dress, it saves somebody turning up in a bridesmaid's dress and looking and feeling hopelessly out of place.

Expense

When you've got everything arranged for the date, time, place, and people your child wants, sit down and work out exactly what you are going to do, and what you are going to feed them on. A lot of this will be determined by how much you are prepared to spend, although it must hastily be added that the success of a party does not depend on the amount of cash you put into it. A most miserable party was given by an ambitious Mother who had hired caterers for the food and an entertainer, but far too many children had been asked who didn't know each other, and the whole thing split into groups of children playing amongst themselves and refusing to be organised. One was left wondering who the party was being given for, herself or her children. The best thing to do is firmly allocate yourself a sum of money and stick to it, and don't be tempted into buying expensive prizes and take home presents. If you are a fantastic cook and bad at decorations, allocate the main

A clown cake baked in a hired mould

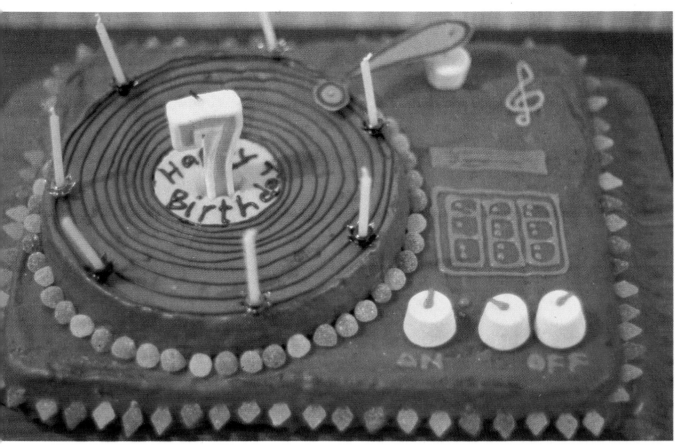

(*above*) An idea for a Disco party;
(*below*) A suitable cake for a girl who enjoys ballet

part of the budget to food, and really go to town on the birthday cake (see page 48 for basic cake mixtures), but if your bent is getting the party going straight away with games and you enjoy it, concentrate on these and get some good prizes for them. You still don't need to spend a lot; in the next chapter there are some suggestions for small cheap presents that appeal to children and different ways of wrapping them, so that they look different and attractive. When deciding on the food you are going to have, remember that things you have cooked yourself will work out much more cheaply, and are really much nicer. The recipes in the food chapter are basically very simple, and shouldn't defeat anybody, and there are plenty of ideas for birthday cakes. Obviously, if you are working, you may not feel like cooking too much yourself, but either way remember that children don't eat a lot at parties, so don't overload yourself, and try to keep a balance between sweet and savoury. Allow yourself plenty of time for the shopping, and hide everything well out of sight from prying eyes and eager fingers. Remember to get plenty to drink, children consume quantities at parties. Any preparation you can do a day or two before to save a last minute rush is well worth it. The day of the party you want to look as welcoming and relaxed as you can, and you won't if you are frantically slicing potatoes for chips minutes before that first guest arrives. Check any

arrangements the day before if you are organising films, entertainers, or outing, and make sure you have plenty of cash if you are taking them out and it looks like becoming expensive.

Help

How much you have to do on the day of the party depends largely on how many children you are going to have, and of what age group. Also a lot depends on how ambitious you are being in the arrangements. If you can, do organise some help; a lot of emphasis is placed on this in 'Ideas', but it does make sense, and pays dividends for your peace of mind. Younger children will have their Mothers with them, but by the time they are about four they will be able to be left at parties, and this is an age when there might well be trouble. Courage fails as Mother departs through the door, and if you can, have a contact point for each child. It sounds over cautious, but you don't want the experience one person had – almost literally holding the baby for two hours whilst Mother disappeared into town shopping. She returned to find a sobbing child and a fairly distraught hostess who had had nobody to help her and was at her wits' end. Nobody's fault; a usually cheerful four year old had unpredictably felt unable to cope. Sadly, this sort of episode can ruin a child's pleasure in parties for quite a while. Then there was the poor child who developed asthma in the middle of the Punch and Judy show (much to his rage), and had to be taken home because his Mother's car had broken down. Fortunately there was an extra pair of hands to hold the fort whilst he was safely delivered home. So be prepared for a crisis, ten to one it won't happen, but you never know when it will.

Clear the decks

Prepare your house for any crises too; again it sounds fussy, and as though you are going to spend the whole day wrapping china up and storing it away, but it does make sense. You don't want a hundred small fingers groping for Smarties or matching cards round your precious ornaments, or Postman's Holiday played in and out of rooms with your chairs and tables just in the path of the letter-posters. Push all the furniture against the wall, and be brutal if you like, lock the doors of any rooms that you don't want the children to go into and take the keys out of the locks. Be careful, on the other hand, to remove any keys from doors that you *don't* want locked, small children have a nasty habit of turning tempting keys; two little girls once locked themselves in a bedroom and had to be removed by the fire brigade. They could quite easily turn the key one way, but not the other. It was a most dramatic and successful form of entertainment, if somewhat unnerving for the poor hostess to see a ladder being hoisted up to the bedroom window to rescue her guests.

Blowing bubbles fascinates all ages

Safety first

Protect the carpet with a sheet if you have to feed everyone in the dining room; and newspaper placed on the table with an old sheet on it, and a cloth on top of that will soak up spilt orange quite successfully. PVC tablecloths are good at protecting the table, but a mug of spilt orange will travel a long way very quickly, so have a few old cloths handy for mopping up. A few sticking plasters for odd wounds and witch hazel for bruises, should see you through any first aid you need to give, and do please make sure all fires are guarded. It is, in fact, illegal to have an unguarded open fire with children around, so it is best not to run the risk and have one in the room that children are playing in. If you have a room that Mothers can sit in whilst the party is in progress and want a fire burning, all well and good, but make sure there is always someone in the room.

Out of doors, make sure that your gate is latched and fastened securely; place a large heavy obstacle against it if you are in any doubt about the safety of the catch. Everyone must have experienced that heart-lurching moment when their back is turned for a second and the child is out and down the road. Remember too, that any water in the garden is a potential death trap. Two year olds have drowned in two inches of water by falling flat on their faces, panicking, and inhaling water in their struggles to get up. If all this sounds alarmist, think how many gardens do have a small ornamental bit of water, always attractive to a child, and always worth investigating.

If you have dogs that are liable to be snappy with strangers, do lock them up for the afternoon. It's a different matter if you are organising a pets' party with supervision, but the devoted family terrier can turn on a small child who perhaps quite unwittingly has annoyed it. Some small children are genuinely terrified of dogs too, so apart from protecting your dog from them, it saves any tears on the children's part.

The final check list

The day before the party run through the final check list, and make sure you have got enough prizes for all the games, a prize for the winner if you are having a party like an Easter Bonnet Party or a Painting Party, and little presents to take home, if you feel that they are necessary. Most children certainly don't expect to go home empty handed nowadays, and it's up to you how much you are prepared to spend. Balloons are a must, so get plenty of these, and buy a balloon pump, you'll find it is worth its weight in gold. Check that you have enough candles for the cake, and that all the table and room decorations are ready; if your older children are helping you they will probably need a gentle last minute nudge to ensure everything is in hand. You'll need drawing

In the party mood

pins, sellotape, and Blutack and scissors, paper and plenty of pencils for all the paper games. If you are having music have a list of the musical games you are expecting to play by the gramophone and make sure you have the right records. A spot check with the older children will ensure you have the latest hits for a disco party, and if anyone is bringing their own records, see that they are labelled clearly with the owner's name. If you have a piano and can play, it's one of the best ways of getting little children to unthaw and get in the party mood. Even if you can't play yourself, persuade a musical friend to come along, it's never any trouble for anyone to do something they enjoy doing, and everyone loves getting children to sing.

The party table

You can lay the table in the morning and then it is out of the way; put a cloth over it so nothing gets spoiled, and label each child's place for them. You and your child will have to go into conference over this, as he will want to sit next to his friends, and if the first you are going to see of them is when they come home from school, it saves any embarrassing last minute squabbling, and hurt feelings on the part of the guests. Don't forget that little children may well need extra height on their chairs, and pillows without pillowcases do very well. If you are extra cautious you may like to put polythene on the pillows and a cloth over that, but on the whole if children are trotted off to the lavatory regularly and a watchful eye kept for any suspicious fidgeting, there won't be any accidents. One mother of four sons always had a large polythene bowl ready under the sideboard in the dining room where they had tea, one of her guests was once violently and unexpectedly sick in the middle of tea, and she's always been prepared since – unnecessarily as it has turned out. Mothers of small babies will appreciate it if you have some polythene bags for the odd used nappy, and a pack of disposable ones in case anybody forgets to bring a spare. If you can get some extra pelican bibs, and spout feeders for tea time, and borrow the odd high chair or two, it will make life much easier. When one is packing up to take a baby out for the afternoon it's all too easy to leave something behind, so the thoughtful party giver will have prepared for this.

The food

The food you have probably cooked ahead and frozen, if you can, so remember to take anything out in plenty of time. It's no bad idea to keep a list of things as you put them in, it's infuriating to go to a lot of trouble cooking something, and then weeks later find it nestling in the bottom of the freezer. Get any sandwiches or bridge rolls spread and covered in cling wrap, mix the drinks, and get the hot food ready to cook. If you are preparing a picnic to take out remember spoons, a sharp knife, sugar, plenty of drink and mugs, and paper napkins and wet cloths, and a towel for drying hands. A box of paper handkerchiefs is useful, and take an insulated flask of tea or coffee for yourself and your friends. Don't forget rugs and groundsheets either, and little picnic chairs if you like sitting in comfort. If you aren't used to organising picnics it's quite amazing what you can leave behind. The minimum of china for all parties of all ages is the golden rule, if you count the number of plastic or paper bowls and cups that end up on the floor and then mentally change that into china you will see the wisdom of this. Children hate breaking anything in somebody else's house. If you have got any Mothers and helpers coming, lay their tea up on a tray to have in peace and quiet in another room if they wish, but they will probably want to stay and help you pass round food and pour out drink. A group of ten two year-olds will have ten Mothers in tow, and a chance for women to eat tea that they haven't cooked themselves makes most of them surprisingly greedy, so have plenty for them too. Two teapots and two kettles keep the tea flowing – and a lot of that will get drunk in an afternoon. If your party is at lunch time or later in the evening, and adults are kindly coming to help you out, it's a nice touch to have a drink to offer them, it's more than likely you will all need it.

Arrival

When the children arrive they may well be a little shy and apprehensive, so launch them quickly into a musical game or an old favourite, but don't force anyone to join in. A bunch of balloons tied onto the gate or the doorknocker makes the house easy to pick out; particularly helpful if you live in the country and directions for 'the cottage on the left after the post box' might not be quite clear enough. By the time the children get to ten, and especially if you have something more adult like a disco party, the girls will want to prink and preen in the bedroom, so lead them upstairs to take their coats off and perhaps comb their hair. It makes them feel deliciously grown up. One Mother had forty children to an evening party and posted one of her friends upstairs handing out cloakroom tickets and hanging coats up for the girls as though they were going to a dance. This small touch transformed them into instant young ladies and they loved it.

Presents

A thorny question is always what to do with the presents that children bring to parties. With perhaps six children arriving at once, and eagerly handing over their gifts, your poor child will be so snowed under that he will be quite unable to appreciate one present before moving onto the next. If there are only a few children, and they have all come back from school together, then opening everything will be a novelty and take up the first

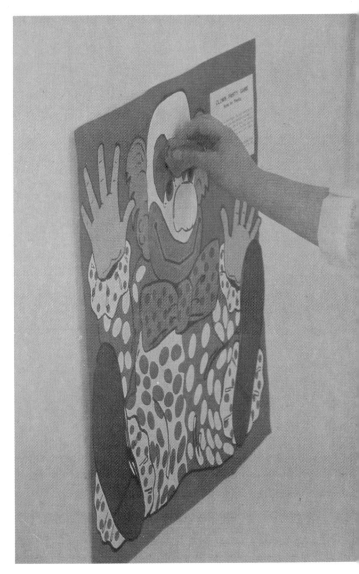

twenty minutes or so of the party. There may even be a new game opened that they all want to play. If on the other hand, you have twenty three year olds to a party, there is going to be no way you can open all the presents at once, so have ready some pieces of paper and sellotape, and write each giver's name on it and stick it on the parcel if it is not accompanied by a card. Thank the child warmly, and then after the party is over and everyone is feeling a little flat, open the presents in peace and quiet, and keep a note of the contents of the parcel. You can then thank the Mother at a later date, or give her a ring. It can be hurtful if one has spent a lot of time choosing something not to have it acknowledged. Make sure your older children thank their guests as they get each parcel. Present giving at parties seems to have got out of hand in recent years; the most expensive and enormous things get given, yet it's much better not to be too lavish. Don't forget the old favourite – a box of chocolates. It's quite a treat for a child to have a box all to himself for a change.

Pinning the nose on the clown

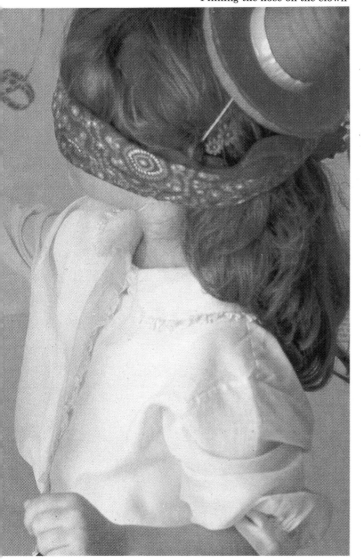

Games

When the games start you will bless yourself for having planned and prepared them all beforehand. It's no good expecting all the old favourites miraculously to come to mind on the spur of the moment, twelve pairs of expectant five year old eyes can chase all thoughts from your head. Prepare a list of all the games you are going to have – in the 'Games' chapter (see page 57) you will find plenty of ideas for every age group. List them according to whether they are team games, competitive activity games or pencil and paper games, and try and vary them to keep their interest. Run down the list and assemble all the equipment you need beforehand, particularly if you are out in the garden; nothing's more irritating than having to dash into the house all the time for forgotten items. Double check to see you have got everything if you are going on a Nature walk (see page 33), or anything that is going to take you a long way from home. Get all the clues set up for a treasure hunt before they come, the objects ready on a tray for Kim's game (see page 74), and the smells labelled or the objects to be squeezed and guessed at stuffed into the tights. The more games you have arranged the better, and always have plenty in reserve. You don't want to be left with ten minutes at the end of the party with nothing to do, and a feeling of rising panic and fifteen eight year olds to amuse. With good planning, however, no one should run out of steam, and even if this is your first attempt at a party all should go well.

Prepare a list of games beforehand

The next one . . .

Finally, when the last guest has gone home you can breathe a self-congratulatory sigh of relief that all went just as you had planned because you were so splendidly organised. In fact, the party was so successful that you are already starting to plan the next one. . . .

CHAPTER 2

ALL THE TRIMMINGS

The party trimmings – invitations and decorations – are usually the bit of party giving that most people find hard to enthuse about doing themselves. When you've gone to the trouble of cooking a lot of food, decorating the cake, and organising the games, the last thing you feel you want to do is to spend time making invitations and decorations for the room and the table. If it is originality, however, that you are looking for in your parties, you have a head start if you make things yourself, and many of the ideas given in this chapter are so simple that the children can help you do them. They love doing so, although you may find yourself finishing off projects, so don't be too ambitious and ask them to do too many. If the initial outlay on materials seems costly, remember that if you have three children who are all going to have parties you can use the stock again and again, and it will probably work out cheaper in the end. Even if you haven't the energy to do a lot of room decorations, do try making your own invitations, especially if you have chosen a theme for the party and want to carry it through. It sets the final stamp of individuality on your party.

Fancy dress

As so many people are often stuck for ideas for fancy dress, included in this chapter are some simple ideas for costumes that the children will enjoy wearing. Good home dressmakers can raid the pattern books for ideas and they will probably have plenty of pieces of material that can be put to good use at last. Don't forget – none of these ideas is expensive or difficult to make, an evening or two will see you through, and the results are well worth the effort.

Prizes and presents

Prizes and presents are the big attraction at any party. Children love getting things to unwrap, and as the word 'competitive' seems unfashionable at so many schools nowadays, they don't often get the chance to compete in something and win a prize. No-one minds losing too much at parties either. Keep an eye on things, however, and if it looks as if one child is going to steal a march on the others, redress the balance by getting him to help you work the gramophone or help organise a team game so that the others get a chance to win. You'll have to be pretty clever to do this without his noticing, but it is worth a try. Don't make all the games competitive either, or the fun of playing a game for the sake of it will disappear. Some Mothers don't give prizes at all, and there is nothing wrong in this; it certainly saves money,

but most children like the chance of winning a prize or two. If you've invited a lot of children and the majority of games are team games, don't attempt to give each member of the team a prize, but have a sweet dip of assorted sweets. Cover a dish with crepe paper and tie round with string, cut a hole in the top, and allow the winning team to dip their hands in to pick a sweet out (a). Put a little thought into wrapping the prizes and presents too – as an original touch will be appreciated by the older children, and can transform a little gift into something really exciting.

a

Try making some of the following ideas, it's relaxing and satisfying; if it's a wet day switch on the wireless, make a mug of coffee, and see what you can achieve.

Invitations

Getting a party invitation is so exciting for a child, and as it's the first indication of how good the party might be, try making them as original as possible. In Chapter I there were the best ways to hand them out, but some invitations may still have to be posted. The GPO, in fact, do accept pretty well anything by post, and whilst this won't include painting the invitation on the side of an elephant and expecting it to be delivered, it does mean you don't have always to think of paper, cards, and envelopes. A carpentry minded Father once cut out some initials from plywood with a fret saw, painted on the invitations, and posted them. One boy was thrilled to get his invitation painted on a large stone – all of the stones were delivered by hand except for this one, so although it was heavy, the cost wasn't prohibitive.

Most people, however, haven't the time and inclination to launch into ambitious projects like these, and the ideas that follow can be done by anyone with a little time and patience. None of them is too complicated, and you can always get the children to help you. Even if you aren't artistic, these designs should prove quite simple, and if all else fails you can trace from pictures in books or magazines, using greaseproof paper. If you have a lot of invitations to do, it's best to make a template – that's a shape in the design you are using, and trace round it each time, to get consistent results.

Your child can make simple invitations himself by cutting out pictures from magazines or newspapers and sticking them onto squares of card, leaving room to write the message alongside. Packets of sticky shapes can be bought very cheaply, and effective pictures made from them by sticking them on cards. Designs and pictures can be drawn on squares of coloured gummed paper, cut out, and stuck on a card.

The variety is endless, and starting with the youngest age group, the one year-olds, here are some ideas to start you off. You need some card, a pencil, glue, sharp scissors, and coloured felt tip pens, or coloured pencils. So have a go, you'll be surprised at what you can do.

One to two years

Initials

Buy some sheets of thin cardboard in whatever colour you choose. Draw a bold solid initial about 12·5 cm (5 in) high for each child on to the cardboard, cut it out, and write the invitation on one side. It is a good idea to buy some envelopes first; stationers have a selection of sizes, so choose a slightly larger size than normal, and make sure no initial is bigger than the envelope. (**b**)

Ribboned cards

You will need sheets of thin white card, and narrow pink and blue ribbon for these. Make a template of the figure one, draw and cut out the required amount of 'ones' then thread pink or blue ribbon through the top of the cards, tie in a bow and write the invitations on one side in pink or blue. If you don't want to be sexist, do them all in a bright colour like red, and buy a metre or so of red ribbon. (**c**)

Candle card

Make a template of a candle, then cut out the appropriate number. Colour the flame yellow and write the invitation on one side. (**d**)

b

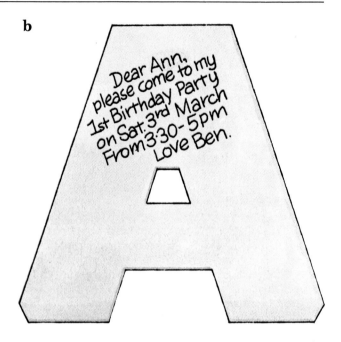

f

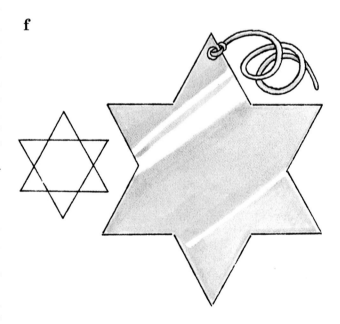

Bangle Card

This doubles up as a teething ring for the guests! You will need some plastic bangles in pink or blue, pink or blue ribbon, and card for labels. Cut out a label for each child, write the invitation on it, and attach to the bangle with the coloured ribbon. (**e**)

Three to four years

A star or moon card

Use this as an invitation to the Fairy revels (see page 30). You will need: thin white card, a can of gold or silver spray or tin foil, and silver string. Spray one side of the card gold or silver, or stick a sheet of tin foil onto one side. On the other draw

a star with six points or a crescent moon. The star is done by drawing two triangles of the same size on top of one another (see the diagram), and the moon is made by drawing a half circle round the bottom of a jam jar (f). Cut out and write the invitation on the card, and thread a loop of silver string through a hole at the top so that the child can hang it up. When you are making these cards make sure you do them on top of plenty of newspaper – the spray goes everywhere.

Teddy Bears' picnic

Your local market will probably have a stall selling remnants of fur fabric, and stuck onto card this makes a lovely teddy bear invitation. Stick the remnant on one side of the card, draw the designs with a template on the other, and cut round it. The bear needn't be anything more complicated than shown in the diagram. (g)

Balloon messages

A simple idea that can be used for any age group. Buy assorted balloons and blow them up. Now write the invitations in felt tip on the side, let them down, and pop in an envelope. Alternatively you can write the invitation on a piece of paper and put it in the balloon. On the back of the envelope, write 'blow me up and pop me'. Older children will like this, but it's not so much fun for the younger age group.

Pink and blue party

Self explanatory – have blue card for the boys and pink for the girls, and tie a pink or blue bow on each if you like. Pink and blue envelopes for the cards can be bought from stationers.

Five to seven years

Entertainers

If you are lucky to know of a joke and trick shop, buy some invisible ink and write the invitations in this. Or write them in lemon juice – if they are held in front of the fire the message will scorch and can be read. Don't forget to write the decoding instructions in ordinary ink on the bottom of the card! Alternatively, stick a sheet of black poly-thene onto a piece of card, and draw shapes of top hats on the other side. Cut them out, make a slit in the plastic by the brim of the hat (making sure there is no glue directly underneath the slit), write the invitation on a piece of paper and slip it into the opening. (h)

Zoo outing

Cut out animal shapes from card and write the invitations on the back. If you feel that you can't attempt a whole shape, just draw a lion's head and make a mane by sticking strands of yellow wool round the face. (i)

Film show

Issue the invitations in the form of a cinema billing such as: 'There will be a showing of . . . at 3.30 pm on Saturday . . . , by courtesy of the manager (your child's name). Admission free. Refreshments pro-vided in the interval'.

Nature walk

Get your child to decorate the invitation card with pictures of flowers, birds and trees, or stick feathers and decorative grasses round the edge. You can cut the cards out in the shapes of leaves or flowers; choose a bold shape like a sycamore leaf, place one on the card and draw round the edge of it. It looks very effective if you use white card and draw a green line round the edge.

Lunch party

Use pieces of paper and fold them in half. On the outside write your child's name and address and the time of the party, and inside write out the food you are having in the style of an hotel menu.

Painting party

Send out the invitations in the shape of artists' palettes with authentic looking dabs of paint on one side and the invitation on the other. Or do as one Mother did, and send each child a brush with their invitation written on a luggage label, and tied onto the handle. Each child brought his brush to the party, used it, and then took it home with his paintings.

h

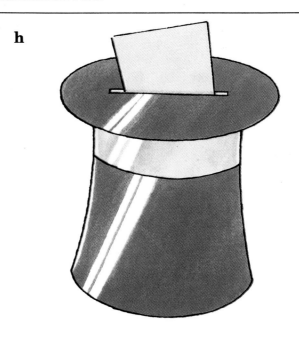

i

Wool chase

If you have an old, out of date map, stick it onto a piece of card, and then cut out squares about 10 × 10 cm (4 × 4 in). Draw a red dotted line on the map, wiggling along a route, then continue this line across the other side. You could start the invitation with something like: 'Follow the wool chase on Saturday . . . with . . . Assembly point . . . State the suitable order of dress – you don't want anyone turning up in sandals on a muddy day.

Pony riding party

If you can find any of those engaging little cartoon characters of riders and their exploits, cut them out and stick them round the edge of the card. Or draw a large horseshoe on the card and write the invitation inside the 'U'.

Easter Bonnet party

Lovely for the children to do. Get them to draw fantasy hats on cards, or use pieces of material to make a collage, and stick scraps of ribbon and lace (or lace paper mats) on as decorations. Write the invitation on the back.

Eight to ten years

Theatre outing

Write these invitations like theatre programmes, folded, with the information inside. Or you can go along to the theatre in advance and buy a programme for each child and pop it in an envelope with the invitation. This saves buying programmes at the theatre, and whets each child's appetite for the show.

Barbecue party

Buy enough meat skewers (available from hardware shops) so that you have one for each child, draw some sausages or chops on brown paper, then cut them out and pierce them on the skewer. Write the invitation on a piece of paper, and skewer that too. Put in a long envelope.

Football match

The boys can cut out pictures of footballers from newspapers for you, and stick them onto cards. Give them a free hand, and they will have a lovely time sticking on football results and well known names as well.

Don't forget to ask people to reply promptly if they can, as this is one case where you do want to know how many are coming, so that you can draw up teams, and fill any vacancies.

Sports events

Cut-out photographs make a very effective invitation background for this outing too; there are always plenty in magazines or newspapers.

Fireworks party

The children can draw pictures of rockets and catherine wheels, and stick little gold stars (bought in packets from stationers) falling down to earth. Glue spread onto the card and then sprinkled with glitter dust makes showers of golden rain, and one little girl made some wonderful Guy Fawkes figures by cutting out pieces of material and sticking them onto a card.

Easter party

Make the invitations out of card in the shapes of eggs, and tie a ribbon round each one. Buy some rolls of the coloured ribbon that sticks together when you wet it, as it saves you tying a lot of little fiddly bows. The children can decorate the card with felt tip pens, or you can buy some sheets of wrapping paper with an Easter pattern on it, and stick it on a sheet of card before cutting the egg shapes out.

Christmas Eve party

If you are going to hand out the invitations yourself, save all the lavatory paper inner rolls you can, and make crackers out of them. Buy some red crepe paper and some wire ties for freezer bags. Cut lengths of crepe paper about 10 cm (4 in) longer than the cardboard roll and wide enough to cover it. Wrap the roll in the paper, stick it securely, and then pinch in each end with a wire tie so that it looks like a cracker. Cut the ends of the crepe paper into a fringe. Write the invitation on a piece of paper and put it inside the roll. Another idea is to get some scraps of material and make miniature Christmas stockings about 5 cm (2 in) to 8 cm (3 in) long. Felt is ideal for this as it comes in bright colours and has non-fraying edges. It can even be stuck together if you don't feel like sewing. The invitation can be written on a piece of paper and popped inside the stocking.

Bring and buy sale

The children will need to be told on the invitation to bring their old toys and books with them, and if you feel you don't want to buy toy money, you can make your own out of cardboard. Write 1p, 2p, and 3p boldly on each coin, and either send the children some money to bring with them or have it ready to hand out as they arrive.

Disco party

You can make these invitations as garish as you like. Use clashing colours; try writing the invitation in black on a bright pink card, and decorating it with black music notes. Or the children can cut out pictures of pop musicians and stick them on the card. The envelopes can be painted bright colours and little gummed stars stuck onto them.

Decorations

Artistic people will have lots of ideas for decorations, but most people will find that they don't know where to begin, so here are some things to do that are gay and colourful, aren't too difficult, and again, shouldn't take too long to do.

The first thing the children see on arrival is the front door, so get a large sheet of paper and write on it 'Welcome to the Party' in a bright colour with a broad tipped felt pen. Or put something along the lines of 'Hello Tom, Emily, Josie, etc., welcome to Henrietta's party', and tie a bunch of balloons on the door knocker or door handle. If it's an outdoor party you won't need to decorate the house; you hope the weather will hold and nobody need come indoors very much. If you are having an evening barbecue, fairy lights strung in the trees look very pretty at dusk, and you can buy special long burning candles for use out of doors that are citronella scented to help keep the insects at bay.

Indoors, decorations can make the room look bright and colourful, especially at winter and evening parties when things need cheering up. If you are giving a party over the Christmas period, the children can stick up streamers and paper chains they have made themselves; and make coils of foil by winding strips round a pencil and then gently pulling it out. You can either cut narrow strips of tin foil or buy a roll of tinfoil ribbon. Make some little choir boys to go on the table. Cut cardboard lavatory rolls in half, put a circle of red crepe paper over it with a strip of a lace paper mat for a frill at the neck, and then glue a table tennis ball on the top. Draw a little face on the ball with a felt tip pen (**a**). Santa Claus can be made the same way, but omit the lace collar and give him a cotton wool beard and a red crepe paper hat. (**b**)

Holly with berries on it is expensive to buy, but find some holly leaves and spray them gold and silver. Tie about four small branches together with red ribbon and hang them up. Larch tree cones on small branches sprayed gold and silver look very pretty in a vase with a single red candle in the centre. A fruit hoop is very effective for any party; for Christmas use satsumas, but when they are out of season red and green apples are very striking. Get a large plastic hoop in red or yellow. Thread thin coloured twine through the fruit, and tie a big knot in the end. Now tie the fruit onto the hoop with varying lengths of the twine and suspend the hoop over the table from the central light fitting with four pieces of strong string. (**c**)

You can hang masses of wrapped sweets from a hoop too, or tie a lot of balloons on it for a lovely table centre piece. If your child has one of those construction sets with rods and blocks in it use them to make a 'washing line' of cards. Place a rod and block at each end of the table, tie a length of string across them, and hang the cards on the string (**d**). You can always stick the cards round the edge of the dining room door frame with sellotape or Blutack and put any up as they get given at the party.

Another effective thing is a decorative tree. Stick a bare branch firmly into a base of oasis in a vase. Oasis is a green sponge block base for flower arrangements and can be bought from most florists. You can spray the branch gold or silver and hang whatever you like from the twigs. The children can help with this rather fiddly job. At Christmas hang glass balls from the branches, and miniature crackers, but at Easter hang up a little hollow chocolate egg for each child and one or two little fluffy chicks. If you've the patience, thread coloured chocolate beans on to different lengths of black cotton with a strong needle and hang from the branches. It looks lovely, but you do need a lot of beans and a bit of time.

You don't need to put all the decorations on the table, and there are several things the children can help you make that are very simple and effective. Buy some shiny foil paper and make simple spirals and lanterns. The spiral looks

a

d

f

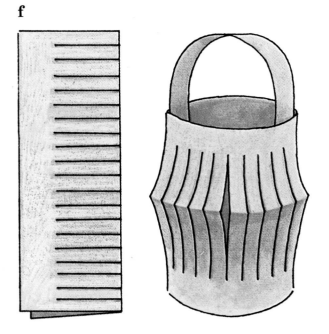

b

c

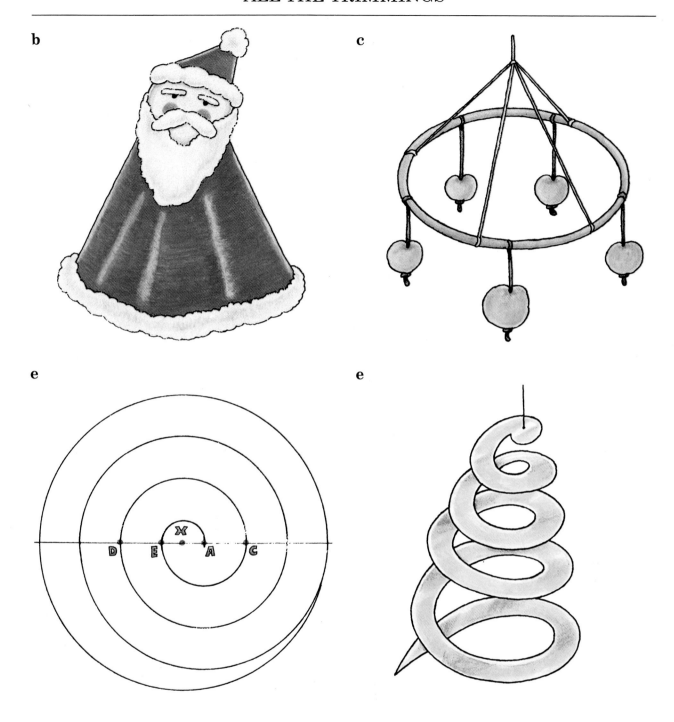

e

e

complicated to do, but if you follow the diagram it is quite easy. You need some compasses for this. Draw a line on the back of the foil. Place the point of the compass at X and draw a semicircle from A to E. Now put the compass point at A and the pencil at E, and draw a semicircle from E to C. Put the point on X again and with X to C as the radius draw a semicircle from C to D. Now use A as a point again and repeat alternatively to make the spiral as big as you like. Cut out and hang up. (**e**)

Everyone must have made lanterns at school, but most have probably forgotten how attractive they are, and how simple to make. Use fairly stiff coloured paper. Fold in half to make a rectangle, and make evenly spaced cuts through the fold to stop about 1 cm ($\frac{1}{2}$ in) short of the edge. Open out the paper and glue the short sides together. Stick a paper handle over the top and hang round the room (**f**). Other things to make that you can hang round the room are stars and moons. They look very pretty if you cut them out of foil paper in different sizes and colours, and if you are having a winter party use plain white paper and paint them in luminous paint. You can cut your child's name out in large separate letters, paint them in luminous paint and string them across the room. They

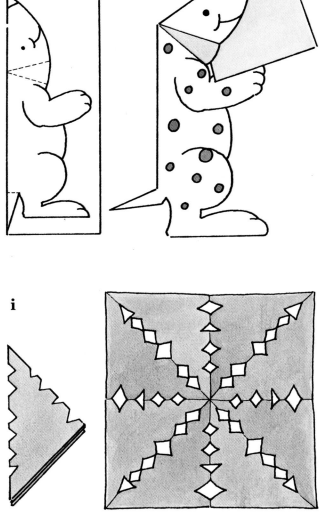

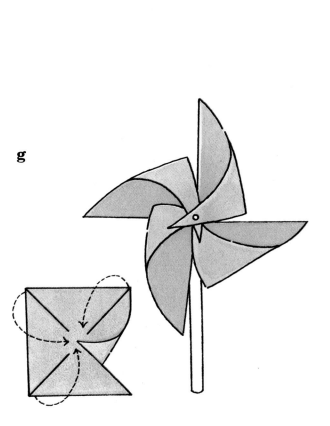

glow in the birthday cake and candle-light.

Young children love windmills and it is really very easy to make your own. They can be put in a vase and then handed out to play with in the garden after tea. Use a stiff coloured paper, draw a square on it, and then make cuts from the corner to just short of the centre. Bend alternate points to the centre and fasten with a pin pushed into a plant stake (**g**). With older children, particularly girls, paper flowers are a great success. Make one for each child and put it on their plates with a bow tied round the stem. They can take them home afterwards. Buy plenty of sheets of coloured tissue paper, and some florists' wire and green crepe paper. Now make a template by cutting out a circle from card about 15 cm (6 in) in diameter (you can make this smaller or larger if you prefer), and cut out about eight circles for each flower. Scallop the edges of the tissue paper circles with the scissors then place them on top of each other, pierce the centre with a 'stalk' of wire and bend the end of the wire back to keep it in place. Fluff out the layers of tissue and bind the wire in the crepe paper.

Another attractive idea is to make a little cardboard animal for each child. Again, very simple to do. Fold some white card in half and draw an animal outline on it so that its backbone is along the fold. Cut out, colour, decorate, or write each child's name on it and stand by each child's plate or round the room. A little begging dog to hold a place card is always very popular. (**h**)

When you are having a day-time party, remember that cut-out motifs from tissue paper can be stuck on to the window panes with great effect. Either single patterns or a frieze can be made; it is just a question of how you fold and cut the paper to produce the patterns. For a single motif fold a square or circle of tissue paper about four times to produce a triangle (**i**). Now cut out a bold pattern from the edges and gently unfold. A frieze is made the same way except that a rectangle of paper is folded in a zig zag fashion, cut and opened out. Don't attempt anything too fancy, a few snips will produce a lovely pattern. Instead of sticking these on the window you could suspend them across the dining room, they look very pretty moving in the heat of the room.

Paper from children's presents can be used again

Prizes and presents

Now for the prizes and the presents – some ideas on what to buy, and some original ways of wrapping them and distributing them. A lot and little is the best rule. There are plenty of small things in the shops that can be bought very cheaply, and department stores often have assorted baskets of small toys, especially at Christmas time. It's a good idea to lay in a stock of these if you know you have a party coming up. Stationers, gift shops, local branch post offices, newsagents, they all have a good selection of small presents. The following is a list of just some of the things that are always a success with children. Note pads, pencils, unusual rubbers, rubber pencil tops, tiny packs of cards, badges, finger puppets, little pocket mirrors, plastic jewellery, bubblebath, bath cubes, stickers, small farm animals, any kind of false appendages like rubber noses, lips and ears, pencil sharpeners, 10p pieces, miniature paint boxes, small books, enamelled rings, packets of stamps, packets of flower seeds, packets of gummed paper shapes, single jumbo felt tip pens, small china animals, and of course, packets of sweets. It is impossible to give all the presents that can be found, but the above will give you some ideas for both sexes.

For take-home presents you may want to spend a bit more, depending on how many children are at your party. Try and make the present seasonal, or tie it in with the theme of the party. A bunch of summer flowers from the garden after a party in the garden or a batch of small chocolate eggs in a cotton wool nest after an Easter party is appropriate. After you have taken the children on an outing, however, and probably spent quite a lot of money, it does seem rather unnecessary to give them all a present. Perhaps a balloon, or a postcard of the zoo or the museum you have been to, but there's no need for more. Children are always impressed by quantity, so if you give them each a balloon, a piece of cake, and single sweet or two, you need only a small gift for them to take home. Wrap them in brightly coloured crepe paper, it's cheaper than wrapping paper, and buy a roll of contrasting ribbon. Paper from children's presents can be saved and used again – press a warm iron on the wrong side and it is as good as new. Girls love a little touch like a single fresh flower sellotaped on to the parcel. The gifts don't have to be wrapped in paper if they are tiny, they can be put in circles of material cut out with pinking shears and secured with an elastic band or tied with sewing thread. Don't forget that white tissue paper secured with coloured ribbon and

25

matching coloured writing looks very striking, and cut out flowers and animals from old Christmas and birthday cards can be used to decorate the present. If the presents will fit into them, make little sacks by running a machine round the edge of small rectangles of coloured hessian to make a bag. Thread string round the top, and paint the child's name on it. You can do the same with old material if you can't find hessian.

Have the presents ready and waiting, but out of sight until it is time to go, and then hand them out at the door as each child leaves. Don't forget your own child! The prizes, however, can be distributed in different ways. A good idea is to have two boxes, one for boys and one girls, if the party is mixed, and then you know the children will get something suitable. Try putting everything in a

Three clowns

box, and letting them take a lucky dip, but don't have sawdust, it'll go everywhere. Instead, have a dip that is like the sweet dip; the children pop their hands in through a slit of crepe paper. Another way to add to the excitement is to attach strings to all the presents, put them under a cloth, and then the children pull a string to get a prize. For bigger children a deep sack that they have to grope around in to get a prize is fun, and another thing to do is to number all the prizes, have corresponding tickets and have a mini-tombola (without the element of chance of winning). Pop all the prizes in a box, the child draws a number and takes the matching prize. All this takes any possible element of favouritism out of prize-giving; although, however hard you try to vary the gifts, there is always something that is wildly popular, and that everyone wishes they had won.

Fancy dress

Finally, some suggestions for fancy dress that will give you some ideas for your children, whether it is for your own party, or someone else's. None of them needs expensive materials, and all allow the children to be mobile when the novelty has worn off, and they want to play active games. If you manage to think of some refinements of your own, do, the ideas here are basic, but require little work.

Alice in Wonderland
A party dress with a white apron over it, an Alice band in long hair hanging straight, and a pair of striped socks, make this simple outfit.

Night time
Make a long, sleeveless tunic out of a dark blue material, and stick on tin foil cut-outs of stars and crescent moons. Make a large cardboard star to put on the child's head, and secure with elastic.

Mrs Mop
Do the child's hair up in a scarf with the knot on top of the head, put on an old dress, give the child a sweet cigarette to smoke, and get them to carry an old bucket and mop. This is a wonderful costume for small boys if they can be persuaded to wear it.

A wet day
Make a long tunic out of net and stick on large drops of 'water' cut out from clear cellophane. Ask the child to wear Wellington boots and carry an umbrella.

A bee
The child wears a black leotard on which you have stitched bands of yellow ribbon. You can tie a black scarf over their head with the knot at the back, make antennae out of pipe cleaners, and give them a pot of honey to carry.

A domino
White tights and jersey, or black tights and jersey are needed for this outfit. Make four large contrasting spots out of thin cardboard, and sew onto the tights and jersey, so that you have a spot on each side of the chest, and one on each leg.

A blazing fire
Make a tunic out of bright red or orange material, and get the child to wear red or yellow tights and a red or yellow jersey. Sew or stick onto the tunic tongue shaped lengths of orange cellophane. A head dress can be made by attaching 'flames' of cellophane to a red or yellow hat.

A ghost
Cut up a sheet to fit the child by placing it over his head, then cutting holes for the eyes, cutting it the right length, and stitching it lightly under the wrists. You can paint eye sockets round the eye holes and a twisted, ghost-like mouth. White socks or tights, and gloves complete the outfit.

A poodle
Get the child to wear a white jersey and tights, and then cut strips of black or white fur fabric to go round the ankles, thigh, arms and chest. Make long flaps for the ears, attach to a hat and tie a red bow on top of the hat.

A gipsy
A gay skirt with plenty of petticoats, a bright shirt, some hoop earrings and a spotted handkerchief to tie round the head are all you need for this outfit. Give the child a wicker basket to carry with bunches of heather in it.

A scarecrow
Dig out your child's oldest and tattiest clothes, fray the edges, sew on contrasting patches, put an old hat on his head with wisps of straw showing from underneath and you have a scarecrow. Give him a pipe to clench between his teeth, and get him to hold his arms out straight at the sides during the parade.

A blackbird
An all black costume for this one, it doesn't matter how you make it up, but make a beak with a cone of yellow cardboard secured round the head with elastic and put a pair of large yellow washing up gloves on the child's feet.

Twelve ideas that perhaps hadn't occurred to you; and of course there are the usual standbys of cowboys, Indians, nurses, fairies, clowns and soldiers. A lot of children have costumes for these already and are quite happy to wear them to parties. They may not win a prize for the most original outfit, but what does it matter as long as they enjoy themselves?

CHAPTER 3

IDEAS

When you have decided, or your child has pressed you into giving a party, you will want to make it as worthwhile an event as possible. Anybody can gather a few children in the house, play a few games with them, feed them and send them home, but it takes a little energy and initiative to give an original party. You needn't be over ambitious: as said before, children are satisfied with very little, but a different idea that lifts the party out of the ordinary can make it so much more enjoyable, not only for the children, but for you too. Instead of dreading doing a formal birthday tea and worrying that ten children are going to wreak havoc in a small house, why not take them on a nature walk, or with bicycles to the park and give them a picnic afterwards? A present to take home, a competition or some races, and an invitation beforehand transforms an ordinary event into a party. Your child, too, will enjoy something different; by the time they are six or seven most children will have gone to dozens of similar parties with everyone wondering secretly if it was worth it. Most children's great friends at school are the same age and there will be a series of parties throughout the year, so if *you* can think of a different idea at a different time, think how popular this will be.

Avoid anything too complicated; it can be torture for busy working mothers to have to run up a suitable fancy dress; and most mothers want to do their best for their children. Everyone knows it's the mother's efforts on the whole, and not the child's. If you do decide on a theme for a party that needs a lot of preparation do give yourself and the other parents plenty of notice. The invitations need to be sent out at least two weeks in advance, and then no one will hear with a sinking heart the words: 'Mummy, I've been asked to Louise's party the day after tomorrow and I've got to go as a pretty fairy'.

As children get older they appreciate more originality and planning. Young children, all children, love dressing up for example, but there are plenty of ways to do this without wasting time and money. A two year-old won't enjoy a trip up the river, but will relish bringing his favourite bear to a party and feeding him party food. It helps one to enjoy the party more at that age if you bring along for comfort someone you know.

You will probably find that as your child gets older he/she will want to have single sex parties. Those boys in the playground are not going to have the privilege of being asked to your eight year-old daughter's birthday party – and girls are similarly eliminated from boys' get-togethers. In a way this makes giving a party easier; it is less complicated to devise a theme for girls or boys to build the party on, than trying to fit in with ideas for both. Outings, of course, are equally popular with both sexes, and can be a marvellous way of entertaining both at once without aggravation. Of course, this isn't the rule of thumb, children mix happily at all ages, but you will find your child will know what he wants to do, and who better to ask? It's their party, and you are just the organiser. In spite of this, you hope to have some wonderful ideas, and it is at times like this, when requests are being made from all quarters, that your wits desert you, and you fall back on giving the conventional party. In this chapter there are some suggestions for doing something different that you can consider and put forward to your child. Could you not for instance take two close friends on a special trip or outing, and then have a small conventional party later in the year? Even if you give the latter, introduce a theme, or serve the food in a different way and play games afterwards, and it will make it a party they will remember. Don't worry that everyone will latch on to the same thought at the same time; each person has their own way of interpreting things, and the way you and your child decide to have your party will make it individual enough. Children have such an enormous and refreshing capacity for enjoyment that your amateur efforts will still be greatly appreciated, and all the trouble and effort that you took in arranging a party with a difference will be worth while.

One year-olds

To be honest, parties at this age are usually for the Mother's benefit and not the child's, although as outlined in the chapter on 'Games' (see page 57), this time *can* be put to good use. Whatever you do, don't ask too many babies. It serves no point whatsoever; the children cry and get irritable, and the mothers worry that their babies are not at their best. So spare yourself the effort, and keep the numbers down to a minimum. Had you thought of this as an opportunity to get the family and godparents, if they live near enough, together? They will appreciate it so much, and there will be no need for entertainment, they will be too busy admiring your baby. If you have a housebound relative nearby, perhaps think of taking the baby there, with a few things in a bag, and getting her to ask a neighbour in for tea as well. This sort of visit can give immense pleasure; it shows you have thought and cared about someone. To carry this idea a little further, you could consider asking a few elderly people in your street that you have seen in local shops, to the child's party. No need for elaborate invitations, just a few words along the lines of; 'I'm having a few friends in to tea for Sophie's first birthday on Friday, and wondered if you would like to come along?' The old lady you ask has probably stopped to admire your baby hundreds of times in the street, and would be thrilled to have the chance to hold and play with her. Those children down the road, aged four and six, with the working Mother, would they like to come and watch Sophie have her bath, and have tea before you or your husband pop them home? Invitations such as these, initially prompted by a birthday, and often not offered because of shyness, can often be the start of new friendships. The party food needn't be elaborate, perhaps a cake as a focal point with one big slow burning candle on it, and a few biscuits and crisps, and a small present for them to take home.

Spare yourself effort with one year-olds

Two to four years

At this age children notice more of the things about them, and although delightfully uncritical and appreciative, it is worth thinking of a simple theme to run through the party. It needn't, of course, be a birthday party; other occasions warrant parties, and some of the suggestions given can be used for the older age groups and adapted accordingly.

Christening anniversary party

If your child was baptised at about six months, as is customary, why not arrange a re-union of the godparents and the vicar in your house? It keeps everybody in contact with each other, and reinforces the meaning of a christening. Some godparents actually like to remember the anniversary of a child's christening rather than the birthday – an unusual but rather charming idea. One teenager was still getting flowers every year on this anniversary, and as it was in the Spring, a beautiful bunch of Spring flowers used to arrive.

Fairy Revels

This idea depends on whether this is an all girls' party, or a mixed group. At this age, the parties are generally mixed, but if you do happen to end

Jelly, almost a must! (for more ideas see page 43)

up with a group of little girls, this appeals enormously to them. Ask them to come dressed as fairies, and it gives them a wonderful excuse to clad themselves in clouds of net and tinsel, with bows in their hair and ballet shoes on their feet. If you can get word round to their Mothers that there isn't a prize for the best fairy, they will be more than grateful. Not much effort is required to deck out a two year-old as she'd secretly always like to be dressed! Make your house as fairy-like as possible, string Christmas tree lights round the tea room, and make stars out of tinfoil and string them together, hanging them across the room.

Pink and blue party

For girls make it a pink party and for boys a blue, and carry the idea right through the party, starting with invitations. Write these on pink or blue card (sheets of this coloured card can be bought very cheaply from art shops and good stationers)

using deeper pink or blue felt tip pens. Your daughter could wear a pink bow in her hair, and your son a blue jersey and trousers. The table can be laid in a pink or blue theme, most stationers and large newsagents have good selections of coloured paper, tablecloths, mugs and napkins, if you are not fortunate enough to be near a large department store. If you can't find these, buy a roll of coloured crepe paper – pink or blue – and put it down the middle of the table. If you can't get coloured mugs, buy white ones and write the child's name on it in the appropriate colour. Ice little cakes in blue or pink icing, and keep the same colour for the candles. Cut out circles of pink or blue material with pinking shears, pop a few sweets in the middle and secure with an elastic band. Little girls would appreciate pink flowers on the table, and plain fizzy lemonade can be coloured pink or blue with food colouring. Be careful, however, blue is not an appetizing food and drink colour, and should be used with caution. The possibilities for this idea are endless, and you can be as elaborate or as simple as you like.

Teddy Bears' picnic

As well as being fun for the children this can also be a help in breaking the ice. Send out invitations along these lines: 'Elisabeth and her favourite Teddy bear are asked to a party on ....'. Put a rug on the floor for the bears to sit on; if you have a few children only to the party they can sit on it too, and feed Teddy and themselves at the same time. Teddy can get a balloon tied to his paw on going home; make sure that no beloved bears are left behind. Little girls will like bringing dolls to a dolls' tea party; boys will not be so keen, but have been known to be enthusiastic admirers of dolls' houses; familiar small scale things fascinate children.

Fancy dress party

More aptly, this could be called a 'dressing-up party'. Have a big box in a room filled with old clothes; if you haven't many yourself, ask some friends to help out. Old nightdresses and petticoats, slippers, high-heeled shoes, handbags, and hats; children will wear anything with great aplomb, and love dipping into the box to find something. They may need a bit of encouragement at first, but soon everyone is suitably clad for the afternoon, and if you have any old costume jewellery put this out too as children love festooning themselves with glitter.

Mummies and Daddies

Another dressing-up party for both sexes. Put men's clothing in one box and women's in another and get the children to dress up as either when they arrive.

Alternatively send out invitations asking them to come already dressed as a Mother or Father. No prizes, just a different idea for a party.

Pets' party

An opportunity to give a small party arises if your cat or dog has had kittens or puppies. Ask a few children only to this party, and preferably have it when the animals are older, as well-meaning as they are, young children can hurt pets in their eagerness to play with them. Interest will wane in the puppies or kittens fairly rapidly, but it is a good excuse to gather a few children together informally if you don't want the expense and trouble of a full scale party.

Pet's party

Five to seven years

The five to seven year-olds are beginning to get more sophisticated these days, and like a party or outing you have arranged that offers them a change from the usual party. The suggestions given here can, of course, be used for older age groups, but one word of warning; for outings for this age, keep them small and manageable, or enlist the help of friends. Over excited children can be very hard to control! Taking children of this age out is a responsibility too, and you need eyes in the back of your head crossing roads. Potentially dangerous things such as firework parties, swimming parties, and bicycle rides to the park for games should be undertaken with great care, with plenty of adult supervision, and if you have any doubts about coping with a party of this kind, the golden rule is – don't. Best to leave these ventures until children are older.

Entertainers

This must surely be one of the easiest ways, although relatively expensive, of giving a children's party, and from the age of five upwards all children love magic, conjurors and puppets. If your child has a friend the same age, suggest sharing this type of party. Very often they are at the same school, and share the same friends, so you halve the cost and effort, and hold the party in whoever's house is the most suitable. This party is easy to arrange. Sit down with a current copy of the GPO's Yellow Pages (or the local paper) and a pencil and paper and list all the suitable names and numbers. Look under 'Entertainers', which will in turn lead onto 'Puppets and Puppet Theatres' and 'Musicians and Theatrical Supplies'. Have ready the date of the proposed party and jot down the services they offer for the age of the children, and the cost, and don't enquire further away than you have to, otherwise you will find yourself paying a heavy surcharge for travelling expenses. Once you have booked a suitable performer, confirm it forty-eight hours before the party and make sure he has a contact number for you. Another thing, and something that is sometimes overlooked, be careful not to engage someone who is too well known in the area: children notice if they have heard a joke or seen a trick done. This type of party is most successful, and the entertainer usually makes a point of singling out the birthday child – this makes it very much 'their' afternoon.

Film show

Twenty to thirty years ago there was a spate of home movies parties, but these seem to have gone out of favour somewhat. A pity, as this can be one of the best ways, and relatively cheap, of entertaining a group of children. The two to four year-old group will find it a strain to concentrate for a long period of time, so rather than make you feel as though the whole thing has been a waste of time, save it until the children are older. If you take your own films all well and good; have you ever thought of showing a film of your family on holiday – but run backwards? Everyone will roar with laughter at the sight of you running backwards out of the sea, getting backwards into the car and disappearing up garden paths the wrong way round.

If you haven't a projector yourself, perhaps you know a friend who has one, and would kindly come and operate it for you, as films can be hired for home showing at little expense, and two short cartoons would be marvellous for children. To find out about hire, look in the GPO's Yellow Pages under 'Film Libraries' and 'Film Distributors' and ring to see if they have anything suitable. Make sure you know the type of film the projector will take, and the length of time you want it to last. To be on the safe side, have a few games up your sleeve ready to play – home movies have a nasty habit of going wrong at the crucial moment.

(*above*) Watching puppets
(*below*) Zoo outing

Zoo outing

Most children have been to zoos by this age, but it is great fun going with your friends. The same advice holds, keep the group small and manageable and therefore more enjoyable. Try going off season, it's less crowded and there's less likelihood of losing anybody. If the zoo has a fun fair attached make absolutely sure of your policy before you go. No rides, or a few, but stick to it, because this sort of thing can become horrifically expensive with even a few children. It's a good idea on the journey to the zoo to compile a list of what they want to see, and then precious time isn't lost lingering over obscure birds and animals. Take a simple tea in a bag; and the children will all want an ice-cream before the day is out. Find out other peoples' feeding times too! Most of the animals have feeding times put up outside their cages, and try not to miss the sealions!

Picnic party

The joy of this is it can be held indoors or outdoors, and is suitable for a small house where there may not be much room for sitting large numbers. It also saves on preparation of tables if you are a working Mother, and has another bonus: children love it! Wrap up little sandwiches and sausages, sausage rolls and pieces of cheese in cling wrap; have a bag of crisps, a biscuit or two for each child, and a piece of fruit and put them all into paper bags, and label each one with a child's name. At tea time each child takes his bag to a rug spread on the floor, and eats his food. Swapping may well go on, but they enjoy this, and you can bring in the birthday cake when they have finished their

Picnic party

meal. One golden rule is to keep them sitting down, children wandering around with food in their hands can create a dreadful mess.

Lunch party

Not only is this the sort of party that children enjoy, but mothers appreciate too. Arrange for the children to come at about mid-day, and be collected by 2.30 pm to 3.00 pm. A little detective work helps here in finding out likes and dislikes, but a choice of hamburgers, fish fingers, sausages, baked beans, chips and crisps is always acceptable, and the pudding need be no more than jelly and ice cream, or pieces of fruit. Satsumas are great favourites, and most children love grapes. If this food sounds rather unimaginative, remember that some children, particularly the younger ones, may not have been out on their own to lunch before, and familiar food will help them to overcome their shyness. For older children you can be more ambitious. Write out menus and take orders as in a restaurant, and serve them at the table; they love being able to choose from a written menu. Paying for it with toy money makes it more realistic too, and even children who are 'pickers' will probably eat a hearty meal.

Nature walk

If the weather is good, and you live in the country this is a lovely way of amusing a collection of children. If you live within a short distance of country, you could combine this outing with a bus or train ride. So often, sadly, the weather conspires to bring this sort of outing to an end, but equipped with wellington boots and anoraks, the children will love sloshing through the mud. What began as a nature walk won't end as one, but hot drinks and hot snacks at home will warm everyone up. For your nature walk give everyone a carrier bag, and a list of what you want them to look for. Some things that children like collecting are stones, feathers, leaves, and anything unusual, and depending on the time of the year you can get them to find catkins and pussy willow, holly berries and mistletoe. Some of them won't have a clue what they are looking for, and if you aren't too sure yourself about some of the things, take a handy pocket nature book with you. A pair of field glasses and a groundsheet or large piece of polythene for weary children to sit on are always useful. The field glasses are good for bird spotting, but are more suitable for a small crowd, otherwise with the best will in the world, not everyone can get a look in. Please be very careful about what you pick; a lot of flowers are protected nowadays, and it is illegal to pick them or attempt to dig them up, and of course, you wouldn't allow the children to disturb birds on their nests or take any eggs. Use this time to infect them with enthusiasm for conservation and inject a little love of the countryside into them – shut all gates, and leave no litter!

Caravan party

Many families now have a caravan, and parked outside the house, most children view it as a little house in its own right. Girls, particularly, love a tea party in a caravan, and if you give them the food ready on plates, and pour out the drink for them, you will find that with their dolls and games, they will be happy for hours. Give them a jigsaw to do, a game to play themselves like Snakes and Ladders, and stay out of sight in the kitchen and you will find that you have a peaceful afternoon to yourself.

Painting party

Best held in the kitchen and with a manageable number of children; you will need to enlist a few helpers for this party. Buy some sugar paper, (still obtainable quite cheaply from art shops), and ask each child to bring a large paintbrush and an overall with them. Have a few old shirts for putting on back to front in case somebody forgets to bring one, and fill some sturdy containers such as clear plastic syrup pots, with water. These can be anchored to the table with a piece of Blutack to stop spillages, or a stone dropped in the bottom of each one to make it heavy.

For paint, invest in three tins of powder paint in the primary colours, red, blue, and yellow and mix them in empty yoghourt cartons. The children can mix the colours in bun tins. Your ingredients are now ready for a painting party, and with plenty of newspaper on the table and floor the children will happily paint pictures. They work with astonishing rapidity at this age, so if you are able to supplement the sugar paper with some scrap paper begged from your husband's office, so much the better. Invite the children to choose their best picture and pin them up after tea for the parents to view and admire when they come to collect them. It is a good idea to award a small prize for the best effort.

Cinderella and the Ugly Sisters

This gives children a chance to look as hideous and ugly as possible, it appeals to boys enormously and can induce them to come to a fancy dress party of sorts, without feeling too foolish. The Cinderella aspect allows the girls to arrive dressed reasonably respectably if they don't feel inclined to be an Ugly Sister. Imagination can run riot here; there are plenty of hideous masks on the market, and dreadful joke wounds, claws, and scars that can be stuck on.

One enterprising Mother dyed old clothes in clashing shades of scarlet and crimson, and painted wellington boots to look like toes. The paint washed off easily afterwards.

Give a prize for the Ugliest Sister and the best Cinderella – if there is one. Continuing along this theme, if it is an all boys' party (or all girls' too!) make it a monster's party; another chance to frighten the wits out of everybody.

Pony riding party

Judging by the immense popularity of pony rides at local fetes, and donkey rides at the seaside, this is a splendid way of keeping children amused, but you do need a large garden or at least an expanse of grass to trot a pony up and down so that they get a decent ride. You do need to know a little about handling ponies, and if you are a complete novice it really is better to have somebody with you who can give advice and trot the animal up and down. Not only is it unfair on the pony, who is expected to behave with a strange child on its back, but it's also safer for the children. So although this party can't be given by everyone, this is worth bearing in mind by the few who may have obliging friends with ponies, or who own one, themselves, but check first to make sure you are covered by insurance for any accidents that may occur. Older children in the eight to ten year age group, if they ride, are pretty competent and would demand more than an afternoon trotting up and down. Local riding stables may consider hiring you a pony with help, so it is worth a telephone call to see if you can enlist their help.

Television party

No excuses for including this as an idea, because for some people with little space, a tight budget, and busy working days, this presents an ideal way to give a small party, even although it appears unimaginative. A good time to give this party is on the day of the last episode of a popular children's serial. For forty minutes the children will be so engrossed that they won't move, and if you invite three or four at the most, it won't be much effort to feed them, and play a few games lasting half an hour or so. There isn't long between arriving home from school and going home at six o'clock, and if they have a hearty tea as soon as they arrive at your house, they won't need anything on going home. An ideal way to satisfy your child's longing for a party if you really can't manage anything else.

Fish and Chip party

Admittedly not everyone's idea of a party, but for those children whose staple diet isn't one of fish and chips, eating out of newspaper with your fingers is a real treat. If there's a good 'chippie' nearby, and you don't fancy frying chips for large numbers, trail them up there to buy their own, and bring them home to eat their spoils round the kitchen table. Even smaller children will enjoy this; perhaps you could cheat a little and cook some fish fingers at home to slip in with the chips – but they must be wrapped in newspaper and eaten with fingers. Plenty of ketchup and vinegar for those who like it, and wet cloths for wiping greasy faces, and you have a good recipe for a party. Older children can help with the frying if you do it at home; if it's a fine day you could have the paddling pool out.

Easter Bonnet party

This custom seems to have died out rather but in lots of ways it's a much easier party to give than a full fancy dress party, as it involves less work for the mothers of the children you invite. Everyone's imagination really has a chance to get going, and the children themselves have a wonderful time helping to decorate the hats they are going to arrive in. You can use ribbons, bells, bows, paper streamers, fresh flowers, painted half egg. shells, moss, catkins, fluffy chickens, feathers, pictures cut out from old cards, and shapes cut out from felt – to give you a few ideas. When the children arrive at the party have a parade round the room to music, and award a prize to the best, then lay the hats carefully on a bed upstairs out of harm's way, as the children will want to take them home with them afterwards. On the theme of Easter Bonnets, if you live in London, the Easter parade in Battersea Park is well worth a visit, and makes a marvellous outing.

Bus or train ride

In these days, with so many people owning cars, a ride on a bus or train can be a real treat for some children. If you are lucky enough to live near one of the new steam lines that have recently opened, you need look no further for your outing, the children will be enthralled by it all. If you live in the country, a ride from your village to the nearest town, some fish and chips in a cafe, and a ride

Bus ride

back again will be all that's needed if your children are used to going everywhere by car. Train rides, sadly, are becoming prohibitively expensive, but arranging to be met by car at your destination for the return journey could help ease the cost. Provide seven year-olds with a pencil and paper, and organise some I-Spy games, such as the number of pillar boxes to be seen on a busy journey – it's fascinating what a group of children will notice when their attention is engaged. Boys will enjoy car-spotting, and a trip to look at the engine is a must before a train ride.

Wool chase

You can't often have this sort of party, as it does require a lot of space, and a lot of adult energy, but if it's well done, it is a great success. Wool is better than paper, for obvious reasons; paper blows away and is messy, and wool can be tied to twigs or branches. This can be organised if you live near a common or park, or near woodland or forestry land in the country. Again, sadly, it does rather depend on a fine day; even though children are happy to run in the rain, it's not much fun for the adult laying the trail.

Two of you make it less arduous, but set off with a bag of long strips of coloured wool, a nice bright colour like red is best, and tie them to twigs of trees and bushes so that they can be seen clearly, but are not too close together. It's probably best to check with officials first if you are going to lay a trail in a park; the Park's Department of the local council will give you clearance or not. Promise that the children won't do any damage (an adult will need to run with them to ensure this) and it will probably be all right. Don't lay the trail too far ahead, it may get removed by well meaning passers by, and if you can summon up the energy make the trail as long as possible. No prizes for the winners, but plenty of food and drink for exhausted competitors.

Eight to ten years

Now is the time to give the parties and have the outings that you thought would prove too much at an earlier age. The same rules apply though, don't take on too many children, and do have plenty of help. A party is for everyone's enjoyment, including yours, and its misery wondering if you can cope once things are in full swing. Most people, with a little initiative, will be able to organise most of these parties – don't be hesitant in asking anyone's advice, they may be able to tell you just the thing you want to know. If booking at a restaurant or theatre, it's wise to do this well in advance to get the best seats, and confirm on the day; and it's worth checking to see if the exhibition you are planning to see is still on! You will enjoy these trips yourself, and what may seem a monumental task in advance, in retrospect will have been a thoroughly enjoyable outing.

Theatre outing

Children love this treat and if your child has a winter birthday, a pantomime is perfect. Most theatres have half price seats for children and pensioners, so this is a good time to enlist the help of grandparents. If you are taking a lot of children, remember that two rows one behind the other are easier to cope with than a long line. Theatres are invariably hot, and to quench the interval thirsts and avoid queueing take a large plastic container of juice and some plastic mugs. Fill a plastic mug for each child with a selection of sweets and seal the top with foil and an elastic band; these can be handed to each child to be eaten at leisure. Do arrive at the theatre in plenty of time, so that they can all go to the lavatory, and with any luck they will last until the interval and won't have to keep bobbing up and down. Enquire at the theatre if it's a pantomime or children's show, to see if they make birthday announcements; the stage manager arranges this. It's such a thrill to have your name read out. A trip to the cinema to see a good film is something children enjoy too, but somehow it lacks the atmosphere of a theatre outing.

Theatre outing

Barbecue party

Burnt sausages, normally rejected out of hand, will be eaten with relish at barbecue parties. Although the climate can prove the downfall of many an outdoor plan, in this case the party can be moved to a garage, but do, at all times, have an adult around, and with supervision the children can cook themselves bacon, hamburgers, sausages, and chicken pieces on the barbecue. Pre-cook the chicken and sausages in the kitchen, they won't take long to finish off on the open flame and stand less likelihood of getting burnt. If you can borrow a barbecue and have two going, it makes for speedier eating, and if you are lucky enough to have a fine day and have, or can borrow a tent, the children will enjoy eating under canvas. Plenty of drinks and some individual chocolate ice cream bars will round off a perfect children's meal.

Fireworks party

Included with reservations, because although it is so popular, it's also potentially so dangerous unless properly under control, so that before anything else do please make sure that you have plenty of adults around, and that the children are kept at a safe distance from the fireworks. Never allow them to light any blue touch papers, but only let them hold sparklers, and even this at the end of the party when all the fireworks have been lit and there is no danger of any going off – set alight by falling sparks. With the price of fireworks these days it is a good idea to combine with a friend for this; if your children are in the same class at school they will have many mutual friends anyway. If you have room to have a good bonfire (not under any trees, or near wooden fences or garden sheds), the children can roast small potatoes in the ashes afterwards and sip mugs of hot tomato soup round the embers. A bonfire usually means a guy and judging by the October crop of guys in the streets most children are pretty good at making these. They aren't difficult with an old stuffed pillow case for a body, and stuffed tights for heads, arms and legs. Any old clothes you want to go can be used to dress the guy up; skirts can be cut up the middle and made into trousers, and jerseys and hats that have seen better days can be put to good use. Very often there are good local firework displays put on by various church or youth groups, and you can take the children to this instead of arranging your own. Your local paper should have details of anything that has been arranged, about a week or so in advance.

Visit to a restaurant

A lot of restaurants will give discounts for parties, or half prices for children, so it is worth ringing round to see what places in your town have to offer. Children love the novelty of being taken out in the evening, and if it's a birthday party, ask if the restaurant will be prepared to produce a cake instead of a pudding. A ten year old boy was once seen at a small Spanish restaurant having the time of his life – he received special attention from all the waiters, and by the time his cake arrived the whole restaurant was ready to sing 'Happy Birthday'. Spaniards and Italians are very fond of children, and will happily fall in with your suggestions. The best part of a meal out for a child is usually the choosing of the food, and a friendly waiter will often steer them to a suitable dish – it isn't seen as parental interference then!

Visit to a restaurant

River trip

A great success with older children, somebody was heard to declare it was the best party they had ever been to after a trip up the Thames. Find out departure times, and arrange for all children to meet at the starting place – give yourself plenty of time, it takes longer than you think to buy tickets and marshall them onto the boat. Wrap up warmly, it can be bitterly cold on a river, enough to damp even the keenest spirits. Don't let the actual ride be too long, but disembark at a place of interest, or somewhere where there is a park for them to run around in, and remember to take a simple picnic tea and plenty to drink. If there are any accompanying mothers, insulated flasks of tea or coffee are essential to revive them, and a large flask of hot tomato soup for the return journey goes down well on a cold day.

Easter party

A party in the holidays is always fun and you will have the children around to help you get ready. Hard boil a lot of eggs, probably two or three for each child; and to vary the colours, drop a little cochineal in the water for a third of them. leave a third white, and add a few drops of green colouring to the water for the other third. You now have a collection of hard boiled eggs, and when the children arrive they can set about decorating them. Felt tips are very good for this, and have a few containers on the table with little silver and gold stars in them, some tubes of glitter, a tiny fluffy Easter chick for each child, and a stick of glue, such as Prittstick, for glueing on decorations. Ten year olds will be absorbed for ages decorating their eggs, and they can take them home with them afterwards. Give a small prize for the best

one, and a little Easter present for each child like a clutch of small chocolate eggs in a cotton wool nest. Girls will love flowers, and a little bunch of daffodils wrapped in yellow crepe paper and tied with a yellow ribbon is a perfect present.

Garden party

A very successful idea for a girl's party if you are fortunate enough to have a large garden, as children love making miniature gardens. Ask each child on the invitation to bring a shallow box or tin filled with earth, and any other bits and pieces they think would be suitable for making an attractive miniature garden. When they arrive give them each a tablespoon for digging up pebbles or extra earth, and be ready yourself to give a helping hand and supervise the gathering of specimens. Make it quite clear to the children beforehand if there is anything they mustn't pick, and stress that as it is a miniature garden everything is on a small scale, so daisies for flowers, and twigs for trees, are the sort of things they should be looking for. Some children will think of bringing pocket mirrors for ponds, and doll's house people, and will produce surprisingly good results. If the weather is against you, and it is a wet day, you may find yourself gathering armfuls of twigs, leaves and flowers and placing them on the kitchen table in jars for the children to choose from. Award a prize for the best one, but ask the children to cast votes on pieces of paper. If your child's is the best at least she's won democratically.

Christmas Eve party

Although this sounds about the strangest and most inconvenient time to have a party, it can in fact be a wonderful way to fill in the evening before Christmas, for children often the longest time to get through before the exciting business of opening presents on the day itself. If you think about it, there is really very little to do in the way of preparation; the house will most likely have a few decorations and a Christmas tree, and you can include any party food you cook in the Christmas preparations. Any extra expense involved in giving a party is more than likely to be swallowed up with the Christmas budget, and make it seem less painful! If you don't want too much clearing up to do afterwards, keep the games quieter, but you will have a crowd of parents most grateful to you for having a peaceful evening to themselves for the final wrapping up of presents and preparations for the next day. *And* you will have enjoyed seeing a crowd of children having a good time – it will be voted a splendid start to Christmas. Ten year olds would enjoy a carol service, your parish church will probably have one at about 6 o'clock, and you could take them to this after games and tea. These can be packed out, so make sure you don't need tickets if you do decide to take them to this.

(above and right) An expedition to the Science Museum, London

Museum outing

The school holidays often bring a spate of good children's exhibitions in most big towns, and your library is a fund of information on what's going on locally. Sunday newspapers often carry a list of 'What's on' in the holidays and give details of admission and times of opening etc. These exhibitions are usually excellent; being in a group with their friends the children don't feel that they've been dragged along to something against their will. Some places have very good quizzes prepared that the children love doing, but check beforehand, because if you have the energy and there aren't any such quizzes available, it is worth doing one yourself. Keep it simple, more an I-Spy than an intelligence test, but it gives the children certain things to look for, and they will absorb far more of the exhibition than they would do otherwise. A trip to the cafeteria for sausage rolls and drinks, and you have the makings of a very successful afternoon.

Dolls' party

So many girls nowadays have jointed dolls, such as Cindys, that a successful way of entertaining a small group of girls is by asking them to bring along their dolls, clothes and furniture. Three or four children will muster up between them quite a collection of things, and will happily spend an afternoon in another world. It is a good idea to keep this type of party small, and confined to one room, as the small clothes are so easily lost. This sort of party can solve the problem of whether or not to let your daughter take her newly acquired dolls and their belongings to school (where you know they will probably get lost). Ask her best friends back to your house, and you will please everyone.

Pyjama party

If you have this at six o'clock on a winter's evening, by the time they have played a few games, the children will be ready for an authentic 'midnight feast', held in the 'dormitory' (your child's bedroom) with torches and candles giving an eerie glow. Naked flame with children, is of course, potentially a great hazard, but if you follow one or two rules you should be safe. Never, of course, leave them on their own in the house for a moment, even to pop to the corner shop, and don't allow any games in the bedroom where the candles are. Protect the candles by fixing them firmly with Blutack to the inside of a jam jar, so that the top of the candle is inside the jar. One or two torches to flash around are always fun, and the 'feast' can take the form of a picnic tea. After all this the children will probably end up by wanting to play 'Murder' or 'Sardines'. Why all this should be so much fun is a mystery, but it certainly fires their imagination.

Football match

If you live in a village, you will find that the village football pitch can often be used on Saturday mornings or on Sundays for a football game. Contact the parish council to find out the procedure in your area, and whether you are able to use the pitch, as this is a marvellous way to entertain an energetic group of boys. Even if you can't rustle up twenty-two players they will happily play with less, and get your husband or willing fathers to do the refereeing and organisation. At the same time as enquiring about the pitch ask whether you can use the pavilion; the boys can change in there and use the washing facilities, and a tea in the pavilion makes it more authentic. You and a couple of friends can be laying out the tea whilst the men referee, and be ready to come out with drinks and orange slices at half time. In summer you can organise a cricket match but this is generally less popular as there is less chance of participation for small boys – in football everyone has an opportunity to have a 'go'. Draw up the teams beforehand with your son's help; thorough organisation before you get to the ground saves standing around in shivering groups.

Bring and buy sale

Bargain hunting is inherent in everyone, not least of all in children, and this is a good way for them to get rid of their old books and toys and get some new ones in exchange. You can organise it like a proper bring and buy sale, and set up a stall by draping an old sheet over a table and putting prices up on everything. Your child may have some toy money already, but if not, it can be bought very cheaply from toy shops and stationers. It won't go home with the other children and can be used again by your own. Ask every child to bring with them about five toys, books or ornaments that they don't want, and collect all the things on the table. Distribute the money as equally as you can to each child, and then price each object, having prepared some labels beforehand saying 1p, 2p, and 3p. Don't make anything too expensive. After tea, which you can have after setting up the stall, let them shop to their heart's content buying other children's cast offs. They will be like new to the new owner. To fill the stall up, if you haven't many children coming to the party, pop on some small, inexpensive things that you have bought yourself, and a few more unwanted possessions of your own family.

Cooking party

Cooking at school is always such a popular activity, that it is worth thinking about giving a small cooking party at home. But again, keep the emphasis on 'small', especially if your kitchen has limited space, and it helps to be well organised with all the utensils ready and a firm idea of what you are going to cook. Children have very little strength in their arms for beating, so don't choose recipes with a lot of creaming in them (you'll end up by doing it and it's just as tiring for you), but have things that involve measuring liquids, cracking eggs, whisking egg whites, sieving flour, and weighing out quantities. Toffee apples are fun to make, and nice to eat afterwards. Have a look through your recipe books for simple biscuits, or cakes to be baked in little paper cases and if you make bread children love kneading it and watching it rise. Decorating and icing cakes is great fun, so it's a good idea to have a plain cake ready to ice, and a mass of those little sugar flowers and tiny coloured balls for making patterns and pictures with. Bake two smaller cakes instead of one big one, there will be more elbow room for everyone and less squabbling. A first aid tip for any small burns that you hope won't happen – hold under cold running water until the pain has gone, it helps to prevent blisters from forming. They will probably want to eat their results there and then, and if you are clever you may manage to take a lot of the effort out of preparing for the party yourself.

Disco party

A disco party at *this* age? But ten year olds love to feel grown up, and a proper party organised at a later hour is a very superior thing. It has the great advantage of appealing to older brothers and sisters too, so whilst they may be liable to scoff at something else, they may well be only too eager to help out at this sort of party. Be careful not to let them take over and subtly introduce too many of their own friends; ten year-olds are still children however sophisticated their tastes, and teenagers are grown up nowadays. If you are lucky enough to have a play room, and can roll back the carpet – marvellous, you won't have any worries about it, but most houses have fitted carpets, so all you can do is push the furniture against the wall. Now make it as romantic as you can, by having one or two shaded lights, or coloured bulbs in the overhead lights, and drawn curtains and constant music. Tape recorders are perfect for this – it saves you the trouble of constantly changing records, and again you'll find that the children are quite happy to record their favourite songs themselves. Organise a few dancing competitions, and elimination dances if they get bored of dancing by themselves, so don't forget to get one or two little prizes beforehand. Ask the children from 6.00 pm to 9.00 pm, and have a buffet supper about an hour after their arrival.

Barn Dance

The children will like dressing up Western style; the boys can come as cowboys with leather belts and pistols, fringed trousers and stetson hats, and the girls in skirts and waistcoats, with their hair in bunches and painted-on freckles. If you have the room, square-dancing is great fun, you need a good 'caller', and some decent music, but the children enjoy this vigorous sort of dancing and if that isn't a success they can always play games.

Combine this party with a barbecue supper, it's much easier to prepare, the usual sausages and baked beans can be produced, and nobody will notice if you haven't been cooking for days in advance. If it's a fine summer's evening, dancing in the garden is great fun, but make sure your neighbours are warned. It's courteous to do so, and point out that it will be for a few hours only in the early evening – they may even offer to come in and help. This party was once given in London, and the next door neighbour was an American who was only too delighted to come and lend an authentic touch to the proceedings. He came as a real cowboy and thoroughly enjoyed himself!

Caterpillar and Hippo cakes (see page 51)

CHAPTER 4

FOOD AND DRINK

Planning

Children's party food is fun to prepare. They love bright colours and imaginative ideas, and when you have run out of these, the 'bagged' favourites such as crisps and potato rings are always successful. Do try to give yourself plenty of time to plan and cook the food; if you own a deep freeze much of the food can be cooked in advance and frozen. Even the birthday cake can be iced and 'open frozen' on a baking tray.

It is well worth going to the trouble of cooking your own cakes and biscuits; large quantities can be made far more cheaply than by buying them, and you have the added advantage of originality.

Children love tiny bite-sized food that disappears in a gulp; munching your way through a large sandwich can be a disheartening experience if your neighbour is popping in appetising morsels in rapid succession. So keep it small and colourful, and don't fall into the trap of providing too much. Children, young ones especially, are usually too excited to eat much at parties; and although older children can be surprisingly ravenous after a busy day at school, even their eyes are often bigger than their stomachs.

So plan what you are going to eat well in advance, what you will cook yourself and what you will buy, and then set aside a few hours one day just for party food shopping. Aim to get the candles and the paper plates, mugs and napkins that day too, and put the whole lot aside in a box until the party day. That way you won't be tempted into buying unnecessary extravagances that won't get

eaten or used, and will save a frantic, last-minute expedition for forgotten items.

Have the food in a room where it doesn't matter if it gets dropped or trodden into the carpet; if there is no room in the kitchen or it isn't a garden meal, take the precaution for younger children of putting a sheet down under the table. Put the table in the centre of the room, as far away from the walls as possible, and have plenty of wet cloths ready for wiping up the inevitable spills of orange juice. This particularly applies in the case of younger children, and one or two extra pelican bibs are always handy here.

Paper cloths, plates and napkins come in a large variety of patterns and colours, so you may like to link your food to a certain colour. Plastic spoons can be used for ice-cream or jelly and are useful for picnics afterwards, and straws are also very popular.

However unadventurous you may be about the sandwiches, small cakes and biscuits, do try to produce a good cake. It is the centre-piece of the party. And even though the children may not be able to eat it there and then, it can be wrapped in a paper napkin, named with a felt tip pen and taken home.

Produce the birthday cake when the children have settled down in their places, eaten and drunk a little, and are enjoying themselves. Have matches handy for the candles, sing the traditional song, and let the birthday girl or boy cut the cake.

Lay the table and put the food out in advance – a small amount on the table at a time, and make sure the most popular things are evenly distributed. It is a good idea to ask your child whom he

Savoury snacks

The party table

wants to sit next to, and what he wants to eat – he will be more up-to-date with current fads and successes of other children's parties. Then name the places, either with a little card, (your child will enjoy writing these out in different-coloured felt tips, and adding a few decorations) or with a bun or biscuit, with the guest's initial piped on it in icing.

Pop some jelly babies, chocolate buttons such as Smarties, little biscuits with coloured icing such as Iced Gems, and a couple of potato rings on each plate for smaller children, it helps break the ice if they have something to nibble the moment they sit down. Do try to organise some helpers for tea for this age group and if you know a particular child is shy, keep an eye on him or her, since it could make all the difference to their eating or not.

Once you've planned your table and gathered all the things you need, what about the food and drink itself?

Popular food and drink

Have plenty of packets of crisps, potato rings, and other savoury snacks, but open a few at a time or you may find that nothing else will get eaten. Children like starting off with a handful of these. Hot cocktail sausages on sticks, or cut-up chipolatas are certain winners, as is cheese spread, spread on toast, put under the grill and then cut into bite-size pieces. Keep peanuts for older children, since they can cause choking in an excited young child.

Don't make too many sandwiches, since they aren't considered 'party food' by children, and when you do, keep them small and open; children like to see what they are eating. Sprinkle hundreds and thousands, chocolate vermicelli or demerara sugar, onto thinly-sliced, lightly-buttered bread or cut animals out of bread with metal shapes, spreading them with a savoury paste and putting a currant for an eye. Make little pin wheels by spreading buttered slices of white and brown bread thinly with vegetable extract such as Marmite, cutting off the crusts, rolling up firmly and cutting into rounds. All these can be done in the morning, covered with cling-film and put in the refrigerator or in a cool place. Older children often enjoy more substantial things such as bridge rolls spread with egg or mashed banana. For the former, scrambled egg is easier to handle and goes further than mashed hard-boiled egg. Other popular toppings are cottage cheese, peanut butter sprinkled with chopped nuts, and just plain tomato ketchup. Mini hot dogs can be made by putting a hot sausage between two little bridge rolls and passing round a squeezy bottle of ketchup – with supervision! Tiny scones are a great favourite with the older age group, and by way of a change can be

flavoured with cheese. They freeze well; thaw and heat through before serving. Hot food is especially good for winter parties, requires little effort, and is invariably a success.

As a change from the familiar wrapped biscuits, try making your own sweet things. Normally easy to make, large quantities can be produced relatively cheaply. A basic sponge cake mixture can be cooked in petits-fours cases, iced, and a chocolate finger biscuit or chocolate stick such as a Matchmaker stuck into each one. Make little 'mice' by turning out the petits-fours cakes, sticking a piece of liquorice 'boot-lace' in for a tail, a jelly bean for a snout, chocolate buttons for the ears, and silver balls for eyes. Arrange them on the edge of a plate facing inwards, with small squares of cheese in the centre.

Vary your flavours, try making a batch of wafer-thin ginger snaps and black treacle flapjacks – simple and delicious. Omit the ginger in half the biscuit mixture and make a bunch of biscuit flowers. Cut out small star shapes with a biscuit cutter and slide a cocktail stick into the base of

each one before cooking. Fix a sweet such as a Smartie – preferably yellow – in the centre of the cooked biscuits with a blob of fudge icing and plant the flowers into halves of upside-down orange. They don't stay 'growing' for long.

Profiteroles disappear in a flash; there's no need to put too much cream in them for children, just plenty of chocolate icing, and meringue nests can be made by piping meringue mixture in small circles with raised edges and filling them with a few jelly beans when cooked.

Make a jelly, but with a difference. Line the bottom of a mould with jelly babies and pour in the melted jelly mixture, when cool. Have ice-cream, but make it different by pressing two Smarties, for example, into the top of a helping of vanilla ice-cream and piping eyebrows and a smile on with chocolate topping out of a squeezy bottle. Again, make it individual by piping the child's name or initial on the top, or by pressing two hollow mints such as Polos into chocolate ice-cream to make 'eyes', with a half mint for the 'smile'.

Make a tea bread, which is simple and much

cheaper than the bought variety, and doesn't detract from the glory of the birthday cake. Similarly, a chocolate fudge cake that needs no cooking and can be kept for up to a week in an air tight tin is sufficiently different so as to not compete with the main attraction.

All this food will produce great thirsts, so have jugs of ready mixed drinks available. Fizz up plain squashes by adding a bottle of tonic water, and drop food colouring into glasses of fizzy lemonade, letting the children choose the colour they want. Lurid pink, green and yellow drinks result, but they are extremely popular.

Milk shakes can be made by buying packets of milk-shake mixture and beating it into the milk. Any left-over shake can be made into a milk jelly by adding powdered gelatine. Follow the instructions on the packet. Float blobs of vanilla ice-cream on the surface of coca-cola or strawberry ice-cream on the top of lemonade. And do have pots of tea for the mothers, or jugs of iced coffee on a hot day. To make this, just refrigerate jugs of cooled, sweetened coffee.

The cake, of course, is the *pièce de resistance*, and your child's delight will be well worth the time and effort taken to make it. Do remember it doesn't have to be professionally iced to be a success; the shape and the idea are much more important to a child. You don't need fancy moulds either, although you can get or hire frames in the shape of numbers, for example, from better household-ware shops. Make a plain sponge or chocolate cake, or Swiss roll, and ice with chocolate fudge icing. This holds sweets and decorations in place well, and you can pipe names, numbers and messages on it. Ice cakes for young children in glacé icing if there are a lot of chocolate things to eat, because a lot of chocolate is rich for them. Glacé icing can be coloured with a few drops of food colouring and then piped, using a plastic forcing bag. Practise on a plate first if you are inexperienced, and if you fail completely you can dip a fine paint brush into the bottle of colouring and paint a name and message straight onto white icing. The ideas for individual cakes follow the recipes and any bits of cake left over can be used for trifles.

Do look in any good grocer's for cake decorations; there is an enormous variety of shapes, colours and flavours available. Finally do remember it doesn't have to be *too* professional; children are very appreciative of party food!

Lemon and orange squash (*back*); milk-shakes (*centre left*); coloured lemonade (*foreground*); vanilla ice-cream on coco-cola and strawberry ice-cream on lemonade (*right foreground*)

Flapjacks

100 g (4 oz) margarine
100 g (4 oz) demerara sugar
1 large tablespoon golden syrup
1 large tablespoon black treacle
150 g (5 oz) porridge oats

1 Grease a shallow baking tin, 18 × 28 cm (7 × 11 in).
2 Melt margarine, demerara sugar, syrup, and black treacle in a deep pan.
3 Add the oats, and spread mixture into the tin.
4 Bake for about 10 minutes at 200°C, 400°F, Gas Mark 6 until golden brown and bubbling.
5 Remove from the oven, and when slightly cooled mark into small squares while still in the tin.
6 Cut into squares when cool and turn out.

Chocolate fudge cake

225 g (8 oz) digestive biscuits
2 dessertspoons cocoa
125 g (5 oz) margarine
2 tablespoons golden syrup

1 Line a 18 × 28 cm (7 × 11 in) shallow baking tin or an 18 cm (7 in) diameter sandwich tin with grease-proof paper. The cake lifts out much more easily if you bother to do this.
2 Crumble biscuits in the blender or crush with a rolling pin between two sheets of grease-proof paper. Stir in the cocoa.
3 Melt the margarine and syrup in a deep pan, then add the biscuits.
4 Press into the cake or baking tin.

Icing

25 g (1 oz) margarine
2 dessertspoons golden syrup
2 dessertspoons cocoa
2 tablespoons sieved icing sugar

1 Melt together margarine and syrup.
2 Stir in the cocoa and icing sugar. Beat well until smooth. Pour over the cooled cake and put in the refrigerator to set. When set, lift out and cut into squares or slices.

This cake can also be made with left-over trimmings from the birthday cake instead of the crushed biscuits.

Ginger snaps

175 g (6 oz) plain flour with pinch of salt
100 g (4 oz) caster sugar
75 g (3 oz) margarine
2 tablespoons golden syrup
2 teaspoons ginger
½ teaspoon bicarbonate of soda

1 Sieve dry ingredients.
2 Melt margarine and syrup, add to dry ingredients.
3 Roll out very thinly on a floured surface and cut into shapes with a metal cutter, or cut numbers and initials with a sharp knife.
4 Prick lightly with a fork, bake on a greased baking sheet for 10–12 minutes, until golden brown, at 180°C, 350°F, Gas Mark 4.
5 Cool on wire rack.

Omit the ginger from the mixture for the biscuit flowers and colour with red food-colouring if so desired.

Flapjacks, chocolate fudge cake and ginger snaps

Sophie's raisin bread

175 g (6 oz) plain flour
2½ teaspoons baking powder
¼ teaspoon bicarbonate of soda
¼ teaspoon salt
¼ teaspoon mixed spice
1 teaspoon ground cinnamon
50 g (2 oz) raisins
250 ml (½ pint) boiling water
2 eggs
100 g (4 oz) soft dark brown sugar
100 g (4 oz) soft margarine
vanilla essence

1 Grease shallow baking tin 23 × 33 cm (9 × 13 in).
2 Simmer raisins in the boiling water for 15 minutes. Drain well, saving ½ cup of the liquid. Cool.
3 Sieve flour and other dry ingredients.
4 Cream margarine and soft dark brown sugar.
5 Beat in eggs gradually, add a dusting of flour each time to prevent curdling.
6 Add dry ingredients to creamed mixture alternately with raisin liquid, then add vanilla essence.
7 Fold in raisins.
8 Turn into baking tin, bake at 180°C, 350°F, Gas Mark 4 for about 45–50 minutes.
9 Cool on a wire tray.
10 Cut into pieces and butter.

Meringue nests

2 standard eggs at room temperature
100 g (4 oz) caster sugar
pinch of salt

1 Separate the eggs carefully, putting the egg whites in a clean *dry* bowl with a pinch of salt.
2 Whisk until stiff and dry.
3 Sprinkle half the sugar over the top through a sieve a little at a time, beating between each application until stiff and glossy.
4 Fold in rest of sugar carefully with a metal spoon.
5 Using a plastic forcing bag, pipe small 'nests' onto a lightly oiled baking sheet.
6 Bake for about 2 hours at 107°C, 225°F, Gas Mark ½ until crisp when tapped with a finger.

The meringue mixture may be piped in small flowers using a rose nozzle if preferred. They can be made well in advance, and store well in an air-tight tin. On the day of the party fill the nests with jelly beans or assorted sweets.

Scones

225 g (8 oz) self-raising flour
2 level teaspoons baking powder
25 g (1 oz) caster sugar
50 g (2 oz) margarine or lard
pinch of salt
milk to mix
50 g (2 oz) grated cheddar cheese (optional)

1 Sieve dry ingredients.
2 Rub in fat, add the sugar.
3 Mix to soft consistency with milk to give a mixture that sticks slightly to the spoon.
4 Roll out thickly on a well-floured surface.
5 Cut into small round shapes with a cutter.
6 Bake on greased tin on the top shelf at 245°C, 475°F, Gas Mark 8 for about 8–10 minutes.

(right) Sophie's raisin bread, scones, meringue nests and meringue flowers
(opposite left) Profiteroles
(opposite right) Danish orange cake

Profiteroles

150 ml (¼ pint) water
50 g (2 oz) butter
50 g (2 oz) plain flour
pinch of salt
2 eggs

1 Put butter and water in a saucepan and bring slowly to the boil.
2 Remove from heat, beat in well the sieved flour and salt until it forms a soft ball in the pan that leaves the sides.
3 When the mixture has cooled a little, beat in the eggs one at a time.
4 Drop *small* teaspoons of mixture onto a greased baking sheet.
5 Bake at 200°C, 400°F, Gas Mark 6 for about 15–20 minutes until golden brown and firm when the sides are gently pressed.
6 Cool on a wire rack, split and fill with a little cream and ice with chocolate glacé icing

Chocolate Glacé Icing

50 g (2 oz) plain chocolate
2 tablespoons water
125 g (5 oz) sieved icing sugar

1 Melt chocolate with water in a basin over a pan of simmering water.
2 Beat in icing sugar until smooth.
3 Spread on profiteroles using a knife dipped in hot water.

Danish orange cake

100 g (4 oz) caster sugar
100 g (4 oz) margarine
100 g (4 oz) self-raising flour
2 standard eggs

1 Grease a 20 cm (8 in) cake tin.
2 Cream together sugar and margarine.
3 Beat eggs and add them and the flour to the creamed mixture.
4 Bake for 20 minutes at 190°C, 375°F, Gas Mark 5; while the cake is baking make the sauce.

Sauce

2 oranges
1 lemon
1 tea cup sugar

1 Squeeze the juice of the oranges and lemon.
2 Add the sugar and boil until slightly syrupy.
3 Leave the cake in baking tin and pour the syrup over it.
4 Leave the cake for a few days before eating it.

This is a good cake for mothers, and older children appreciate the refreshing taste.

Basic birthday cake mixtures

The following recipes are for birthday cakes, and ideas for their decoration. Both the sponge mixture and the milk chocolate cake are best made in two tins, so use either two deep 18 cm (7 in) round tins or two 18 cm × 10 cm (7 in × 4 in) rectangular deep tins. It will specify which tin to use. Arm yourself with felt tips, a thin sheet of white cardboard, some stick glue, such as Pritt's, and a box of liquorice allsorts, which will be invaluable for making little extras that cannot be made easily out of cake. You will also need a piping bag with various nozzles, bottles of food colouring, a fine paintbrush for painting designs on the icing, and other assorted things that will be specified with each cake. Choose something to suit the sex of the child and the time of the year, for example the basket cake could be made for an Easter birthday and filled with little chocolate eggs and a miniature fluffy chicken for each guest. And if you know that your child has a large collection of model footballers, for instance, choose the football match cake – it will save you buying unnecessary decorations.

For a larger party you will, of course, have to double the recipe and use bigger tins. Be careful with the cakes that are supported on biscuits for their effect – it is better to make two of these rather than run the risk of making a huge, top-heavy 'dog' or 'rocket'.

Swiss roll

3 large eggs at room temperature
75 g (3 oz) caster sugar
75 g (3 oz) self-raising flour
Jam

1 Grease and line a shallow Swiss Roll tin 23 × 30 cm (9 × 12 in) with grease-proof paper.
2 Whisk the eggs hard with the sugar until the mixture is light and creamy and leaves a trail from the whisk when lifted out.
3 Fold in the flour with a metal spoon.
4 Turn into a tin, smooth over with a palette knife.
5 Bake for 7–10 minutes at 220°C, 425°F, Gas Mark 7 until pale gold.
6 Turn on to grease-proof paper dredged with icing sugar, spread with warmed jam of your choice, and roll up.

Don't worry if this cracks whilst rolling up – it can be masked with chocolate fudge icing. It is worth making one of these yourself – it is quite simple to do, and much nicer than the bought variety.

Milk chocolate cake

This is an excellent recipe and is one of the few cakes that can be made equally well by hand, in a mixer, or by food processor.

200 g (7 oz) self-raising flour
225 g (8 oz) caster sugar
½ teaspoon salt
2 tablespoons drinking chocolate
100 g (4 oz) margarine
2 eggs
5 tablespoons evaporated milk
5 tablespoons water
1 teaspoon vanilla essence

1 Grease two deep 18 cm (7 in) tins, either round, square or rectangular, whichever is specified – but not loose-bottomed.
2 Sift dry ingredients.
3 Rub in margarine.
4 Mix together eggs, milk, water and vanilla essence, and then stir in.
5 Beat very well until the mixture is soft.
6 Bake in a moderate oven at 180°C, 350°F, Gas Mark 4 for about 30 minutes. The cake should be springy when pressed with a finger. Be careful not to overcook it, as it will lose its moistness.
7 Ice with chocolate fudge icing (see page 49).

Milk chocolate cake, Swiss roll, sponge cake, pipping nozzles

Sponge

100 g (4 oz) butter or margarine
100 g (4 oz) caster sugar
2 standard eggs lightly beaten
100 g (4 oz) self-raising flour

1 Grease very well two 18 cm (7 in) round or square sandwich tins.
2 Cream together butter and sugar until pale and creamy.
3 Beat in the eggs a little at a time, with a small spoonful of flour to prevent curdling.
4 Sieve the flour and gently fold into the mixture with a metal spoon.
5 Bake at 180°C, 350°F, Gas Mark 4 for about 20 minutes. The cake should be springy to the touch and golden brown.
6 Cool on a wire rack.

Icings

Butter icing

175 g (6 oz) butter or soft margarine
250 g (9 oz) sieved icing sugar

Cream the butter or margarine which has been allowed to soften and beat in the sieved icing sugar until fluffy and white.

To vary the fillings try using a flavoured butter icing. Orange and coffee fillings are good with chocolate icing and a lemon icing and filling give a delicious sharp taste to a sponge cake.

Chocolate add a tablespoon of chocolate powder to the butter icing mixture.
Coffee add a teaspoon of instant coffee dissolved in 2 teaspoons water to the butter icing mixture.
Lemon add 2 teaspoons of finely grated lemon rind plus a dessertspoon of fresh lemon juice to the butter icing mixture *gradually* to avoid curdling.
Orange add 3 teaspoons of finely grated orange rind plus a dessert spoon of fresh orange juice to the butter icing mixture *gradually* to avoid curdling.

Glacé icing

225 g (8 oz) icing sugar
2 tablespoons water

1 Sieve the icing sugar twice to make it really fine.
2 Add the water gradually, beating well after each application.
3 Pour the glacé icing over the cake when it is stiff enough to coat the back of a wooden spoon.

Frosted icing

A sweet, soft icing that can be swirled into peaks.

450 g (1 lb) granulated sugar
150 ml (¼ pint) water
2 egg whites at room temperature

1 Dissolve the sugar in the water, stirring continuously until no granules are left, then boil hard without stirring until it forms a soft ball when dropped into cold water, or at 120°C, 240°F on a sugar thermometer.
2 Whilst the syrup is boiling, whisk the egg whites in a large bowl, until stiff.
3 Pour the syrup on to the whisked whites.
4 Whisk until the mixture is thick and will coat the back of a wooden spoon.

Chocolate fudge icing

This makes an excellent icing that is easy to work with and spreads well. It covers and fills an 18 cm (7 in) sandwich cake generously.

75 g (3 oz) margarine
4 tablespoons chocolate powder (cocoa)
225 g (8 oz) sieved icing sugar
3 tablespoons evaporated milk
1 teaspoon vanilla essence

1 Melt the margarine and the cocoa together.
2 Stir in the icing sugar and evaporated milk with the vanilla essence.
3 Beat very well until smooth.

The birthday cakes

The recipes on this page and page 51 use the basic Swiss roll recipe (see page 48).

Train cake

Chocolate fudge icing
1 packet of chocolate Swiss mini rolls
1 packet of jam-centred whirl biscuits
A sheet of cardboard (thin) obtainable from stationers and art shops
Cocktail sticks
1 packet of chocolate buttons, such as Smarties

1 Ice the Swiss roll with the warm fudge icing (having cut away a piece for the train driver and stoker – see picture). It is easier to spread when warm, but not too hot.

2 Put the roll onto the cardboard after you have cut a strip wide enough to take the 'train' and have painted the rails on it. (Borrow the children's felt tips.)

3 Fix four jam-centred biscuits on the train as wheels, and join mini rolls onto the train and each other with two cocktail sticks as couplings. Make as many of the 'carriages' as you like.

4 Make a little chimney by rolling and sticking a strip of the remaining cardboard into a funnel shape, or use half a mini-roll.

5 Decorate the carriages with the chocolate buttons for windows, and liquorice allsorts for wheels, and put a puff of cotton wool smoke coming from the chimney. If the children have any favourite plastic figures, dot them around the cardboard – they are always delighted to see something familiar.

Christmas Cracker cake

1 Cut the roll in half and make two cylinders of cardboard about 8 cm (3 in) long and the same diameter as the Swiss roll.

2 On a board fix a cylinder to one end of each half of the Swiss roll.

3 Ice the roll with chocolate fudge icing and continue onto the cardboard in a thin layer.

4 Carefully lift the two halves onto a rectangular board or tray that has been covered with crepe paper or foil.

5 Fill the two cardboard halves with sweets, push the two halves together, and spread icing over the entire crack.

6 Make ends for the cracker by making a cylinder out of a length of crepe paper, wiring it and securing it onto the end of the Swiss roll with more wire on cocktail sticks. (see illustration)

7 Pipe messages with glacé icing, and 'cut' the cake by pulling it apart (you may need a fork stuck into the end to do this). Hey presto! All the sweets fall out – remember to remove the card before eating.

Hippo birthday cake (see page 40)

1 Ice a Swiss roll with chocolate butter icing, refrigerate until cold and firm.
2 Cut two chocolate mini-rolls in half, and support the Swiss roll on these to make the legs.
3 Make the head by securing a mini-roll on to the body with cocktail sticks.
4 Pipe two rosettes with white glace icing for eyes, and cut two small triangles for ears out of thin cardboard (or decorate as in picture). Do this before attempting to fix the head onto the body.
5 Secure the head and neck onto the body with two cocktail sticks.
6 Put half a chocolate finger biscuit in the other end of the Swiss roll for a tail.
7 Ice 'Hippo Birthday to you', on the top with white glacé icing.

Caterpillar cake (see page 40)

1 Ice the roll with green fudge or frosted icing.
3 Stick a double row of chocolate sticks, such as Matchmakers, along the length of the roll, putting some at a slight angle so the caterpillar seems to be standing on its 'legs'.
3 Make the head by icing half a Swiss mini roll, securing it onto one end of the big roll with two chocolate sticks and putting two more for antennae. Use two cut pieces of jelly beans (white) or chocolate sticks for eyes.

Rocket cake, perky dog cake and baked bean cake

Baked bean cake

Carefully steam off the labels from two tins of baked beans. Make a Swiss roll and ice with frosted icing, cut in half at the level of a baked bean tin. When the icing has set, wrap the labels round the outside, put foil over the top, and secure with sellotape. Bring the two 'baked bean tins' in and watch their faces! Have candles ready to change them into birthday cakes.

Perky dog cake

1 Ice the roll with fudge or frosted icing.
2 Secure four chocolate fingers into the roll for legs.
3 Cut a Swiss mini roll into four rings and ice with the same icing as the big roll, and stand the chocolate fingers in the four circles to form the feet.
4 Cut another mini roll in half, ice, and secure onto one end of the big roll to form the head.
5 Cut little triangles out of a layer of a square liquorice allsort and insert in the head for ears, and use sweets for eyes. Make the tail by cutting out a thin strip of cardboard, winding it round a pencil and then pulling the pencil through and press into the icing. Or, use a chocolate finger, see illustration.

Rocket cake

1 Ice the roll with frosted icing.
2 Stand it on its end and support with four chocolate fingers or other biscuits stuck in at an angle.
3 Make a cone out of thin card and put on the top for the nose.
4 Pipe with glacé icing or paint designs and messages on the sides.

(*opposite*) Train cake
(*below*) Christmas cracker cake

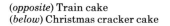

Basket cake

Bake the Sponge or Milk Chocolate Cake in two round tins.

1 Cut the centre out of one round of cake and sandwich the cut cake onto the top of the other half, using the chocolate fudge filling.

2 Spread the rest of the icing over the cake, except for the well in the middle.

3 Pipe diagonal lines crossing over each other to simulate the weave of the basket, using white glacé icing.

4 Make the handle by cutting a strip of cardboard and bending it across the cake, securing it into the icing. Decorate by twisting crepe paper or ribbon round the handle, and pressing sugar flowers into the edge of the cake.

5 Fill the basket with mixed sweets.

Basket cake

(*above*) Birthday clock cake and flower cake
(*below*) Country cottage cake and fruit bowl cake

Birthday clock cake

Use the sponge or milk chocolate cake recipe. Sandwich the two halves together with jam or chocolate fudge icing and ice the outside as desired with fudge icing, glacé or frosted.

1 Pipe the numbers one to twelve onto chocolate buttons.
2 Put round the cake to form the clock.
3 Either pipe the hands to the age of the child, e.g. 3 o'clock for three years, or use Matchmakers as hands.

Flower cake

Use the sponge or milk chocolate cake in two round tins.
1 Draw a flower shape onto a circle of grease-proof paper the same size as the cake. Place the cut-out shape on the cake and carefully cut round the edge with a very sharp knife. Repeat with the other half, so that you have two 'flowers'.
2 Ice with contrasting glacé icing, making one white, and the other pink, for example. Place a yellow sweet such as a Smartie in the centre for the 'eye', or decorate to suit.
4 Put the two flowers on a piece of cardboard at different heights and draw the stems and leaves according to size.

Fruit bowl cake

Use the sponge or milk chocolate cake mixture in two round tins.
1 Cut a well out of one round of cake.
2 Place this remaining hollow ring on top of the other round of cake to make a good rim, securing with icing of your choice.
3 Ice the outside and top of the cake.
4 Fill with mandarin oranges and grapes.

Country cottage cake

Use the sponge recipe or milk chocolate cake in square tins.
1 Trim the cake so that it is higher than it is wide when sandwiched together with icing, and ice the sides, not the top.
2 Make the roof by cutting a strip of cardboard the width of the cake, and then bend it in half to fit the cake.
3 Fix a chocolate-covered mint, such as an After Eight, at an angle to form the open door and decorate with sugar roses.
4 Peel the layers off square liquorice allsorts, cut into four and stick on in groups of four, slightly apart, to form the window panes.
5 Place the cake on a piece of cardboard, draw a path up to the front door, pipe a line of icing and stick halved Matchmakers in for the fence, and make a path with hundreds-and-thousands. Put dolls' house furniture and people in the garden.

Calculator cake

Use the sponge or milk chocolate cake in two rectangular tins.

1 Sandwich together the two halves and ice with the icing of your choice.

2 Pipe a window at the top with the child's age in it e.g. 00000007.

3 Using square liquorice allsorts as the buttons, pipe the numbers and symbols on in contrasting coloured icing. Press into the cake.

Hedgehog cake

Use the sponge or milk chocolate cake recipe in two round tins.

1 Trim the two rounds into oval shapes and sandwich together with icing. Taper one side.

2 Ice with chocolate fudge icing and cover with spines of halved chocolate sticks, such as Matchmakers, leaving the tapered end clear for the face.

3 Insert a black liquorice roll for the snout and two chocolate buttons for the eyes.

Ladybird cake

Trim and sandwich together two rounds of cake as in the hedgehog cake.

1 Ice with red glacé icing, except for the head which should be iced with chocolate fudge icing.

2 Pipe a line across the tapered end in white glacé icing, and a stripe down the back. Press in peppermint fondants or chocolate buttons for spots.

(*above*) Calculator cake;
(*below*) Ladybird cake and hedgehog cake

Football match cake

Use the sponge or milk chocolate cake in two square tins.
1 Sandwich the two halves of cake with icing.
2 Ice with green glacé icing.
3 Pipe out a football pitch with white glacé icing and place the model players on it. A useful idea if your son already has the players!

Number or initial cake

Use square or rectangular tins.
1 Draw and cut the number out of cardboard the size of the cake.
2 Sandwich the two halves together with icing, place the template on top and cut round the outline with a sharp knife.
3 Ice and decorate with halved chocolate buttons or chocolate covered buttons placed side by side along the edges of the number, flat side down.

Butterfly cake

Use two round sandwich tins.
1 Sandwich the two cakes together with icing.
2 Cut the cake in half and place the two curved halves back to back. Cut a small triangular wedge out of the centre of the outside of each wing, and use these pieces to make the head.
3 Ice the cake in a coloured glacé icing and pipe 'veins' on the wings in contrasting icings using a fine nozzle.

(below) Football match cake, number cake and butterfly cake; *(right)* Truffles

And to use those left over crumbs after you have trimmed the cake to the shape you wanted . . .

Truffles

50 g (2 oz) butter
50 g (2 oz) caster sugar
almond essence
75 g (3 oz) ground almonds
2 teaspoons cocoa
50 g (2 oz) cake crumbs
orange juice
chocolate vermicelli, hundreds and thousands

1 Cream together the softened fat and sugar until light and fluffy.
2 Add the almond essence, ground almonds and cocoa.
3 Beat thoroughly, mix in the cake crumbs.
4 Add the orange juice, roll into little balls in the palms of one's hands, and roll in the vermicelli or the hundreds and thousands.
5 Put into petits-fours cases.

The chocolate fudge cake can also be made with left-over crumbs instead of biscuits. Alternatively, put the crumbs in a dish, pour a melted jelly on top and add a tin of mixed fruit. When set decorate with piped cream or custard.

CHAPTER 5

GAMES

Every children's party goes better with organised games; it may be tempting to avoid the effort of arranging them, but you will find that precision timing from the moment the first guest arrives until the last one goes pays dividends. This may sound alarming, but visualise ten or twelve seven year-olds totally out of control in an average size house and you will understand the necessity for military organisation. Remember, too, that the children you have seen pouring out of school shouting and chasing each other may find their confidence sapped at the thought of an afternoon in a strange house, and become uncharacteristically shy unless coaxed to join in some game or another. Similarly, the child whom, up to now, you thought you would be glad to welcome to any party may turn out to be the demon who needs no breathing space, and otherwise he and half a dozen others will be constantly wrestling in heaps on the floor.

The large majority of children, however, love parties, and after some initial shyness, respond and co-operate enthusiastically with party games. Adjust the games you play to the weather, and the size of your house and garden, and have plenty of them up your sleeve. If interest is obviously flagging in what *you* had thought was a particularly good game, don't persevere, drop it, and move on to the next one. On the other hand, if a game is a huge success and everyone is enjoying it, don't be alarmed at the prospect of none of your carefully planned games being played, but continue with it until they tire of it. The children will soon say when they have had enough.

A party has been known to run for two hours with the children playing no other game other than dividing into two teams, dipping into a dressing up box and acting nursery rhymes and charades to each other. Organised by two particularly dynamic little girls, they were a gift to any party giving Mother!

When the games are in full swing, do watch for the one or two who want to sneak off upstairs and play with jointed dolls such as Action Man and Cindy; it can cause a party to disintegrate, as everyone will want to play with them, and precious bits and pieces always get lost. Keep this sort of activity for two or three children who come to tea.

Whatever games you decide to have, have plenty of the equipment you need, as pencils get lost, balloons burst and paper gets mislaid. If you are lucky enough to have a fine summer's day for your party and a good sized garden, have all the games outside, but if you are giving a winter party and have a small house plan your games accordingly. Don't try and play a game of sardines in a three bedroomed house where every available space is used for storage, or organise riotious team games in a room unless you have removed some furniture and anything breakable.

The arrival at a party before the games begin can often be a difficult time, but smaller children, in particular, love musical games, so have the gramophone playing as they arrive and encourage them to join in a singing game as soon as possible, it will help to break the ice. With older children a guessing game or simple game such as pinning the tail on the donkey as soon as they arrive can cause excitement and laughter. The sooner you can introduce these two elements into your party, the better it will go!

In the one-hundred odd games given in this book there will be something for every situation and party. They are divided into age groups, but you will find that some of one group will be equally successful with another. Indoor games can be adapted for out of doors and *vice versa*. There is often an 'in' game at school and the children will clamour to play it. Let them! They will enjoy it all the more. It's up to you as to whether you have prizes for every game, some of them, or none at all, but make sure that the children know before the game begins.

Some of the musical games will be familiar, but are given, as so often the old words and music have been forgotten, and the games aren't played as nobody can remember them at the last minute.

There is plenty here to refresh your memory, introduce you to new games, and help your party to be a great success.

One year-olds

Games at this age are non-existent, or so one thinks. Most babies, however, love being joggled on people's knees, and songs being sung to them.

If you keep the party small, half a dozen mothers can have an enjoyable time singing with a record to their babies and playing with them. Ask the mothers to bring along a favourite toy, and for those on the verge of walking have a baby walker with some bricks in it. Everyone will take great pleasure in encouraging the early walker.

Toys such as posting boxes, and hammer and peg sets are useful to have around, but simple everyday objects like wooden spoons and saucepans make good substitute toys, and try filling a few empty two litre plastic ice cream containers with familiar objects and letting the babies tip them out and fill them again. All babies love tearing things, and as it's a party give them sheets of tissue paper (the cheap white kind that china and glass is wrapped in) and allow them to rip it up. It could keep them happy for a long time.

Babies of this age are, of course, crawling, and it's unfair to expect to sit in your sitting room surrounded by all your things and not expect the children to go crawling after them to investigate. And nobody wants a baby to sit on its Mother's lap for a solid two hours, so be fair and remove all the things that you don't want fingered, bitten and sucked, and then everyone will relax and have a good time. If you have a summer party and it's a fine day, count yourself lucky, as a few plastic washing up bowls filled with water give endless, if somewhat wet, entertainment. Take off their clothes, and let them crawl around with nothing on if it's hot enough, and no one's party things will get spoilt. If you are fortunate enough to have a sand pit, young babies will sit contentedly for hours pouring sand from container to container. They also eat it, and put it over each other, so they need to be watched. The few that are walking at this age will enjoy staggering around trying to pick the flowers!

Although parties for this age group are more for the mothers to show off their babies, do try and use it as an opportunity to encourage everyone to play with babies; one of the best games there is.

Two to four years

At the bottom end of the scale two year olds are sometimes difficult to organise, they lack concentration and lose interest very quickly. Musical activity games suit this age well and they love familiar repetitive songs, but you will find they respond to little else, so don't try to arrange games. They enjoy pottering around and playing with toys more than anything. As they get older they begin to enjoy the spirit of competition, but keep the prizes very small and have plenty of small sweets available as consolation prizes. As yet too young for pencil and paper games they delight in noisy entertainment, but keep it in control with the help of another adult, and older brothers and sisters. It's always helpful to have somebody spare to comfort those who fall over or want to go to the lavatory. No blindfold games are included for this age group as some younger children are genuinely frightened of them, and hate this to be shown up in front of their friends.

Pass the parcel

An old favourite, but still one of the best introductory party stand-bys there is. Choose a small present and wrap in layer after layer of loosely wrapped paper, fastened with sticky tape or string. sit the children in a circle and get them to pass the parcel round to music. When you stop the music the child holding the parcel tears off paper until the music starts again, and the parcel has to be passed on. The winner tears off the final layer to get the present. For the youngest children chocolate covered beans, such as Smarties, strategically placed in the wrapping paper will keep their interest alive.

Musical statues

(*above*) Musical bumps;
(*below*) Hunt the Sweets

Musical statues

More for four year olds, and played in the same
way as musical bumps, except that when the music
stops they have to be as still as possible, and those
who move are out. But don't be too particular,
this age group are inveterate wobblers.

Musical bumps

Another old favourite, but also another winner.
Familiarity never breeds contempt with children!
They jump up and down to music and when it is
stopped the last one to crash to the floor each time
is out. Some children refuse to sit down, but in-
sist on keeping going, much to their pleasure.

Hunt the sweets

Much more exciting at this age than hunt the
thimble. Place small sweets round the room in
various places (make the hiding places harder as
they get older, and extend it to two rooms) and
tell the children to search for them. On finding
them they are allowed to eat them, but must
stand still as they do so. This gives them all a
good chance of success. If you prefer, hand each
child a small container to collect the sweets in and
wrap them for them to take home.

Ring-a-ring of roses

Rather morbidly, this game is supposed to have originated in the days of the Great Plague, when a sneeze signified that one fell down with the dread disease never to rise again. The children dance round for this joining hands in a circle. The words are:

Ring-a-ring of roses
A pocketful of posies,
A-tishoo! A-tishoo!
We all fall down.

Whereupon the children collapse on the floor. Make it competitive, if you like, by saying the last child down is eliminated, but be careful, they probably won't like being out, and will want to go on playing.

(Fast ♩.)

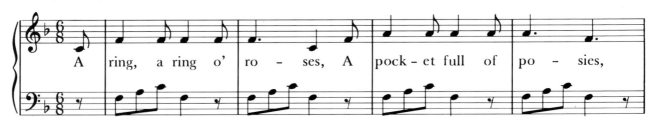

Ring-a-ring of roses

Farmer in his den

Another singing game, and one that is always popular. The children form a circle round one child standing in the middle. An adult sometimes needs to stand with them for encouragement. They then walk or skip round singing:

The farmer's in his den
The farmer's in his den
Hey ho, Hey ho
The farmer's in his den,

The farmer wants a wife
The farmer wants a wife
Hey ho, hey ho,
The farmer wants a wife.

Whereupon the 'farmer' chooses a 'wife' and retires to his 'den', the middle of the circle, with her. Repeat the rhymes and actions substituting wife and child, child and nurse, and nurse and dog, for farmer and wife.
The last verse is:

We all pat the dog
We all pat the dog
Hey ho, hey ho
We all pat the dog.

The dog goes on all fours and is patted – gently – by the rest of the children. One of the children not chosen begins the game again.

Here we go round the mulberry bush

The children form a circle and dance round singing:

Here we go round the mulberry bush,
Here we go round the mulberry bush,
Here we go round the mulberry bush
On a cold and frosty morning.

They then stop and mime:

This is the way we wash our clothes
This is the way we wash our clothes
This is the way we wash our clothes
On a cold and frosty morning.

An adult leads on the second verse each time, substituting a different action each time.

Here are some suggestions:

This is the way we put on our shoes.
This is the way we clean our teeth.
This is the way we brush our hair.
This is the way we eat our lunch.

Make the actions familiar, and you will find that they want to play the game for what may seem to you a remarkably long time.

(Fast ♩.)

Oranges and lemons

Try to be careful that not all the children want to queue behind the 'orange', as so often happens, and the poor 'lemon' is left – seemingly – without any friends. Two children, one an 'orange' and one a 'lemon', make an arch by facing each other and holding hands high above their heads. The rest of the children dance round in a line passing under the arch and singing:

'Oranges and Lemons', say the bells of St
    Clements,
'You owe me five farthings', say the bells of
    St Martins,
'When will you pay me?' say the bells of Old
    Bailey.
'When I grow rich', say the bells of Shoreditch.
'When will that be?' say the bells of Stepney,
'I'm sure I don't know', says the great bell of Bow.
'Here comes a candle to light you to bed,
And here comes a chopper to chop off your HEAD.'

At 'head', the children making the arch trap someone in their arms and he chooses to be an orange or a lemon, queues behind the respective child, and the game continues until all are out.

Oranges and lemons

Lost letters

Another singing game all children love. One child is given an envelope (try and find a brightly coloured one and put folded newspaper in it to make it heavy, empty envelopes have a habit of floating around), and walks round the outside of the rest of the children who have sat down with their eyes shut forming a circle facing each other. They all chant:

I wrote a letter to my love
And on the way I dropped it.
One of you has picked it up
And put it in your pocket.

Whereupon the letter writer drops the envelope and all the children open their eyes to look and see if the envelope has been dropped behind them. For younger children this will be enough, it is their turn to drop the letter, but the older ones will enjoy the added fun of trying to run right round the circle pursued by the letter writer to reach their place safely again.

Cat and mouse

All the children scuttle round on the floor on their hands and knees squeaking loudly, whilst the music plays. On stopping the music 'meow' loudly and all the children have to stop squeaking and be perfectly still to avoid being caught by the imaginary 'cat'. Whoever squeaks or moves is out.

Poor puss cat

All the children sit on the ground, and one child is the puss-cat. The cat goes to each child in turn, meows, and asks to be stroked by a child. He can be as silly as he likes and pull as many faces as he likes, but the other child must be perfectly straight-faced. If the person stroking him laughs, they are out, and become the cat. The cat needs encouragement to move on, so that he doesn't become stuck in front of his best friend.

Where's my sock?

A good game for younger children on arrival. On a large sheet of paper stick coloured advertisements for rooms of furniture torn out from magazines. Try and include a kitchen, a bedroom, and a sitting room. As each child arrives say 'Naughty . . . (naming the child whose party it is) lost one of her socks last night, and it's somewhere in the house, but we can't find it, do *you* know where it is?' and give them a pin to stick in the picture. Mark their efforts, and when everyone has had a turn the one nearest to the lost sock is the winner. It adds to their fun if you actually put a sock in the spot in your house you have decided on in the picture, ie. under the bed, or in a drawer, and get the winner to run and see that the guess is right.

Counting the pebbles

For four year olds who are at play group and may have learned to count. Sit all the children on the floor with their backs to you, and stand behind them with a biscuit tin. Drop at irregular intervals ten or more pebbles (depending on their ability to count) into the tin, and get them to tell you how many you've dropped in the tin. They all try to count out loud, and get very confused. The quantity and speed of pebble dropping can increase with age, but remember how many you have!

GAMES

(Fast ♩)

O-ran-ges and le-mons, Say the bells of St Cle-ment's. You owe me five far-things, Say the bells of St Mar-tin's. When will you pay me? Say the bells of Old Bai-ley. When I grow rich, Say the bells of Shore-ditch. When will that be? Say the bells of Step-ney. I do not know, Says the great bell of Bow. Here comes a can-dle to light you to bed, And here comes a chop-per to chop off your head.

Balloon bobbing

This sounds amazingly simple but affords endless amusement. Pat a balloon to a child, who then pats it to another child. They have to keep it up in the air. Younger children can be allowed to catch it and throw it again.

Balloon bobbing

Copy cat

Sit on a chair facing the children who are sitting in an expectant group on the floor in front of you and explain clearly what you want them to do. You may find this game beyond two year-olds, and have to restrict it to four year-olds, but it's worth a try. Say that as you point to a part of yourself and name it, followed by 'meow', they have to imitate it, but only if followed by the word 'meow'. For example, point to your chin and say 'chin, chin, chin, meow', whereupon they all follow suit. Now point to your eyes and say 'eye, eye, eye', and make sure no one is a copy cat, if they are, they are out. Children love this game, as they love all imitative games at this age and this is a good one for getting them all off the ground.

Follow my leader

Another imitative game that may seem trite to adults, but played with gusto by children. It's a good game to start a party with, as it's non-competitive, and doesn't require any special talents. If you have a willing friend as a helper at the party, fit her in the line about half way, to encourage the latter half of the line of children. With yourself at the head, and a record on the gramophone, jog round the room either skipping, hopping, jumping, running, jogging or walking and get the children to change each time you change. Hop over chairs, crawl under tables, and bob in and out of rooms. They'll follow you eagerly!

Pair them up

Enlist the help of any older members of the family for this game – they can do the donkey work collecting pairs of things. For two and three year olds restrict this game to one room, for four year olds you can be more adventurous and spill out into the hall. Before the party collect pairs of a number of small things like cotton reels, paper clips, hair slides, pencils, rubbers, wrapped sweets, stamps, thimbles, tea bags, sugar lumps, dried peas, anything you can lay your hands on that comes to mind. Have ready a paper bag for each child and pop six halves of pairs into each bag. Hide the other halves of the pairs round the room or rooms (before the party), hand each child a paper bag, and get them to find the matching half and pop it in the bag. First to get a correct collection wins.

Give the dog a bone

A guessing game that doesn't involve blindfolding – especially for the little ones. Draw a picture of an appealing puppy, it doesn't matter about artistic merit – if you really *can't* cope, cut a picture out of a magazine, but there's usually one member of a family who is reasonably artistic. Cut out the picture and stick it on a poster size piece of paper, and on the back of the paper write the word 'bone'. Now draw a realistic lot of bones and cut them out too. Line the children up at the party, and taking it in turns, give them a 'bone' with their name written on it, and a drawing pin, and get them to pin the 'bone' where they think it should be. The child with the 'bone' nearest to the word written on the back is the winner.

Cops and robbers

All the children stand in a circle holding hands, with one child inside (as the cop), and one child outside (as the robber). The cop has to try and catch the robber, but the robber is prevented from going through the circle of children, whereas the cop is let through. The robber has to try and make a dash for it all the time and avoid being caught by the cop. A slighly disorganised game that may get out of hand, but it doesn't matter too much – children love it.

Secondhand shop

One of those hilarious, chaotic games that everyone enjoys playing: younger children love any excuse to dress up, and it doesn't matter if there isn't a winner. Gather together a pile of old clothes of all shapes and sizes; hats, gloves, scarves, shoes, nightdresses – anything will do – and put them all in a large box. At the start of the game put a garment for each child less one (e.g. nine garments for ten children) out of the box in a pile on the floor at one end of the room. Line the children up at the other end, and tell them when you say 'go', you want them to rush to the shop and 'buy' an old garment, put it on, and then rush back to the starting line. The child who fails to get a garment can then help you put out the next pile, now eight things for the nine remaining children. The game continues until one child is left, hung about with strange clothes, as you allow them to keep on what they are wearing after each round.

What's the time Mr Wolf?

You had better be Mr Wolf, it's more fun to be chased than the chaser at this age. Agree on a safety zone for the children, such as a sofa or a rug, and then stalk round the room followed by the party crowd who keep calling 'What's the time Mr Wolf?' If it's any time except '12 o'clock DINNER TIME', they are quite safe, but as soon as you reply with the fatal words in a realistic growl, they have to run for safety to the alloted place. If you catch anyone they are your dinner for the day, and become Mr Wolf – if they want to.

Balloon race

If you have a lot of children divide them into two teams, but otherwise let them play individually. Have one or two large cardboard boxes according to how you are going to play the game, and a large number of blown up balloons. Put the box or boxes at one end of the room and the children at the other, and get them to bat a balloon each into the box at the end. Not as easy as it sounds, balloons are never very easy to control. Two year olds will probably end up chasing each other round the room, but it doesn't matter they will still have fun.

Musical hats

Variations on musical games for this age group are endless, but a very good one for this age is musical hats. Sit the children in a circle and give

them a hat. If you can find anything like a top hat or something different, so much the better. Anything, in fact, that comes over their eyes and makes everyone laugh. Now get them to pass the hat round to music, and put it right on when they get it. The one wearing the hat when the music stops, is out.

Musical arches

Two adults, or two children, (but they will want to play the game more than likely), form an arch, and the children dance round the room passing under the arch as they do so. When the music stops the arch comes down and any two children caught have to queue behind the arches. Continue until all the children are out.

Rhyme mime

This may seem an obvious way of passing the time for the youngest ones, but just because of this it is often overlooked. Sit all the children on the floor in front of you and sit yourself on a chair in front of them. You will have to know your Nursery Rhymes for this one, if you don't, borrow one of the children's books, and read them out. This is all you have to do, and accompany them with suitable actions that you ask the children to follow. For example:

'Little Miss Muffet sat on a tuffet'
(you sit yourself firmly on the chair)
'Eating her curds and whey'
(you eat imaginary food with relish)
'There came a great spider'
(creep around with a dreadful expression on your
   face)
'And sat down beside her'
(sit yourself down again)
'And frightened Miss Muffet away'
(run off with screams)

Little children delight in copying your actions, and you will find this a good time filler.

GAMES

The Cokey Cokey by Jimmy Kennedy

Most people know the tune to the Cokey Cokey, if not, the music is reproduced.

'You put your left arm out,
Left arm in,
Left arm out, and shake it all about,
You do the Cokey Cokey and turn around,
That's what it's all about,
Ooooh, the Cokey Cokey,
Ooooh, the Cokey Cokey,
Ooooh, the Cokey Cokey
That's what it's all ABOUT'.

Substitute left arm for right arm; left foot for right foot, etc., and keep going until the children are bored with it. Stand them in a circle, and with the last four lines get them to run with joined hands into the middle of the circle, and back again.

Three blind mice

One of the children is in the middle of a circle of the rest of them, and he or she is the Farmer's Wife. The children dance round singing:

'Three blind mice
Three blind mice
See how they run, see how they run,
They all ran after the Farmer's Wife
Who cut off their tails with a carving knife'.

Whereupon the Farmer's Wife dashes from the middle of the circle, and tries to catch someone. The 'mouse' then comes to the middle of the circle with the Farmer's Wife and the game begins again. It ends with one victorious child being chased by all the rest. You can either let the Wife do all the chasing or let the mice join in as well.

by Jimmy Kennedy

(Steady ♩.)

Three blind mice, see how they run! ——— They all ran af-ter the far-mer's wife; Who cut off their tails with a car-ving knife, Did you ev - er see such a thing in your life, As three blind mice.

Down on the farm

Great fun, and delightfully noisy for the younger ones. Write a short story down on a piece of paper, bringing plenty of animals with familiar cries into it. It needn't be a very exciting story, the whole point of the game is to make the cry of the animals you mention in the story. It could go something like this: 'It was a fine day, so I took my dog for a walk (they all bark), across the fields to the farm. We passed some cows (everyone moos), and some horses (everyone neighs), and some sheep (baas from the assembled children), etc. Continue for as long as your imagination and patience can stand in this vein, it's immensely popular with young children.

Out of doors

All the singing games can be played out of doors very successfully, but you may find that once the children are out of doors they will be happy to push doll's prams, come down slides, ride tricycles and play in sand pits, and won't need any specific organisation.

As a party beginner, and as soon as all the children have arrived, make a conga line and jog gently round the garden singing a well known nursery rhyme. The children love it, and it helps to get them going.

All change

Spread the children round the garden, and stand in the middle. Call out two names of children who then have to change places, and you try to run to the spot that one of them has vacated. Don't try too hard with the youngest ones; it's just a good way to get them to run about in a fairly organised way.

French tag

The children run around the garden and you chase them, as energetically as their speed demands. When you catch someone tap them on a part of their body, such as the elbow, and they are now the catcher, but have to run holding that part of them you have touched. If you play this with older age groups you can touch ankles, knees and other awkward parts of the anatomy, but for younger children keep to such things as heads, noses, and hands.

Broken bridges

Put two lengths of string across the lawn to represent the banks of a stream, and a fairly wide plank joining the two banks at one point. Get the children to run round the garden and cross the 'river' by the plank. Turning your back to them cry 'Splash', and any child caught on the plank has fallen in the river, and is out.

Five to seven years

This age group begins to segregate itself at parties, boys usually preferring rowdy, physical games and girls quieter ones. There are exceptions of course! You may find that your child firmly announces, as early as six, that no children of the opposite sex are going to be asked, and you can pick the games accordingly. The spirit of competition begins to be strong at this age, but if you believe in fair play for everyone make it perfectly clear at the beginning of each game there *are* no prizes to be won, so that there are no disappointments. Team games begin to come into their own at this age group, but it is a good idea to decide for yourself on the teams, as this saves the pain of being the last to be chosen.

Squeak piggy, squeak

A lively game that everyone enjoys playing, but make sure that the child with the pillow doesn't mind being blindfolded. Sit all the children in a circle, and put a child in the middle, holding a pillow, and with a loose blindfold round their eyes. They then walk slowly towards someone holding the pillow in front of them. (You may have to lead the younger ones gently in the right direction). When they come across somebody, they put the pillow on their lap, and say 'Squeak, piggy, squeak', and sit on them. The selected child, the 'piggy', squeaks as strangely as he likes, and the blindfolded person has to guess who it is. One word of caution here, make sure the children *do* know each other well beforehand, otherwise it gets very confusing. Excellent for children who all go to school together.

Money in a matchbox

This is a good game for each child to do on arrival. Pop some money in a matchbox, tape it up, and wrap it in paper. Hand it to each guest and ask them to guess how much money there is in the matchbox. They can rattle it around to assist themselves. The child with the nearest guess gets the box to take home. For younger children, put sweets in the box.

Sweet bashing

This sounds alarming, but is verified to be a great success! Put a selection of small sweets in a tough paper carrier bag, (put two bags inside one another to make the game last longer), tie firmly at the top and suspend from the doorway by string tied to the handles. The mark won't show later if a nail to hang the bag from is driven into the top of the door frame. Line the children up, and give them each a turn at whacking the bag with a wooden spoon or stick. Eventually the bag bursts and they all tumble for the spoils.

Potato pins

Give each child a potato, and have ready as many pairs of children's woollen gloves as you can find. The more gloves you have, the more people can play at once. Have a saucerful of pins in front of them, and get the children in turn to put a glove on the hand they pick the pins up with, and against the clock see how many pins they can stick in the potato. Younger children will need longer, older ones less time. Very frustrating.

Cats and dogs tiddly winks hunt

Before the party begins, scatter tiddly winks around the house and/or garden. Divide the party into two teams, cats and dogs, each with a leader. Give the leader a container. Send the teams searching, but the only person who can pick the tiddly winks up is the leader, who is 'summoned' by his own side (cats meow, dogs bark). The team with the most at the end wins.

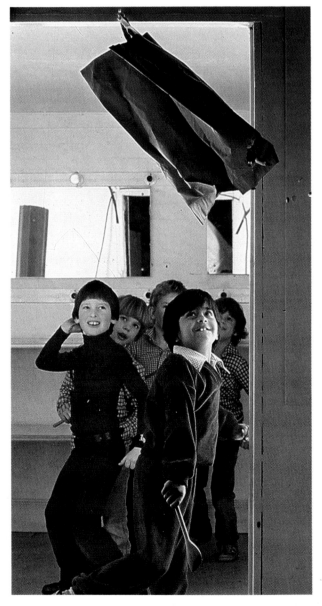

Sweet bashing

Sardines

Eternally popular, and good for people with larger sized houses. One child hides in a suitable place and the others search for him. On finding him they cram in with him. Eventually the whole party ends up in a giggling group under the bed or behind the door.

Nose to nose

A hilarious team game, it's for older children too. Sit all the children on the floor in two lines and give the first one a matchbox lid to fix on his nose. He then has to pass it to the next player and fit it on his nose, using no hands. The first team to complete the line wins.

Busy bees

All the children choose a partner, and spread themselves out over the room with you standing in the middle. You then call out various things for them to do like, 'jump up and down', 'stand back to back', 'hold hands and skip', and they do this unless you call 'busy bees'. When you call this they rush around and find a new partner. During this rush you also try to grab a partner, so they have to concentrate too on not being grabbed by you. The child left without anyone becomes the Queen bee and gives the commands.

Tortoise race

Line all the children up, on all fours, and start with 'Ready, steady, go'. They *have* to keep moving but the *last* to reach the finishing line is the winner. Excellent for quietening everybody down after vigorous games.

Dead lions

Another joy when the party has become too noisy, and curiously enough, immensely popular. The children jump up and down to music, and when the music stops lie on the floor. Anyone who moves is out, and it is now their turn to try and make any of the others move by verbal means only, such as 'There is a spider crawling up your left leg'. No touching allowed, and those who do move are out. It usually ends up with two stalwarts who refuse to budge much to the delight and frustration of the other children.

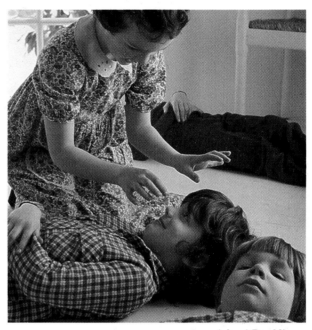

(*above*) Dead lions;
(*below*) Sardines

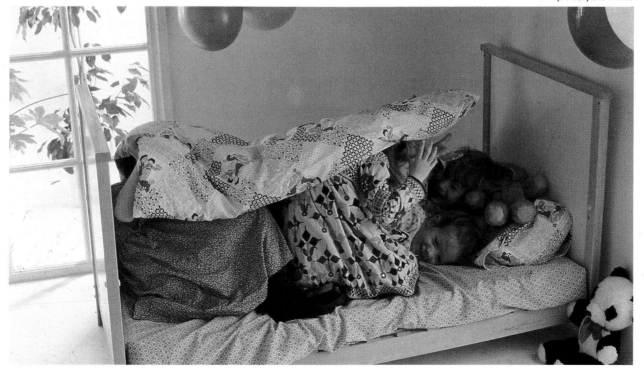

Blowing the ball

Musical mats

Easier to play in most houses than the more familiar musical chairs as only sheets of newspapers are needed. Place five or six newspapers on the floor, spaced round the room. The children dance around to music stepping on each newspaper as they come to it. When the music stops anyone who is on a newspaper is out. Bring the papers in closer together as the numbers get less.

Musical apples

Place apples in various places round the room so that they are accessible but not obviously visible. Have one less than the number of children. The children dance round the room to the music, and when it stops, they rush to get an apple. Anyone failing to get an apple drops out; the apples are collected up and reduced to one less again, and the winner is allowed to keep an apple.

Blowing the ball

Divide the children into two teams, each team with a ping pong ball and each child with a straw. On their hands and knees each child blows the ping pong ball through the straw along the carpet to a finishing line and back again. The first team to finish wins.

Teddy's bedtime

Divide the party into two teams again. Give each team a pair of adult's bedroom slippers, a teddy bear and an unlit candle. One by one the children have to put the slippers on, hold the bear in one hand and the candle in the other and run to a finishing line, where they shout 'Goodnight Teddy' as loudly as they can. On hearing this the rest of their team put their fingers to their lips and say 'Sssh!' as loudly as *they* can. The child then runs back holding the bear, slippers and candle, and the next one goes. The first team to finish, wins.

Ring round the ring

An old favourite, but always very popular. It's a good quiet game to be played after a few hectic ones. Sit the children in a circle and give them a long piece of string threaded through a ring and tied at the ends to form a circle. You stand in the middle of the circle to start the game off, close your eyes and count to twenty. Whilst you are doing this, the children pass the ring around the string keeping their hand clenched over it as they do so. When you reach twenty, open your eyes, and try to spot who has the ring hidden in his hands. If you guess correctly, that person comes into the middle of the circle, if not, you stay in.

Teddy's bedtime

Forgetful Fred

There are plenty of variations on this game, but this is one they all seem to find amusing. Sit the children in a circle, and stand in the middle of them. Say with a very solemn face 'Forgetful Fred has lost his head, it rolled away for many a day, and who picked it up but you . . .' and you point fiercely at one of the children. Silently, and with a perfectly straight face, they have to point to someone else, who then in turn points to another child. Anyone who speaks, smiles or laughs during these silent accusations becomes the person in the middle.

Jigsaw cards

Use as many old Christmas or birthday cards as there are guests. Cut each one into four assymetrically (for younger children the cards may be cut in half). Give each child one piece of each card, and hide the rest of the pieces round the room. The first to find all the correct pieces and make the complete card is the winner.

Match-it-up

Separate a box of chocolate covered buttons such as Smarties into colours, and cut strips of matching coloured wool, thread or coloured pieces of paper – one for each button. Then give each child an equal number of different coloured strips and a container. They must find the corresponding coloured beans that you have hidden round the room. To be eaten then, or saved to take home.

The Tower of Pisa

Have ready a number of square building bricks (about six or seven for the younger age group, and more for the older ones) and a dice and shaker. One child starts building a tower of bricks and the other children take it in turns to shake the dice; when a six is thrown the next child in the line knocks down the tower and begins again. The first child to complete a tower that stands to the count of six with all the bricks is the winner. Increase the number of bricks if it is getting too simple.

The parson's cat

As well as being a good party game, this is a useful game for playing on long car journeys. Sit the children down and explain that they have to name the parson's cat in turn with the letters of the alphabet. So the first child will say something like: 'The parson's cat is an angry cat, and is called Amanda'. The second child may say: 'The parson's cat is a beautiful cat and is named Bob', and so on. When you play this with younger children omit the adjective, seven year olds will manage both. Anyone who cannot produce a name or adjective to the slow count of five, is eliminated.

Musical pillows

Sit the children in a wide circle, each child quite far apart from the next. Get them to throw a pillow to each other as the music plays. When the music stops the child holding the pillow is out. Not so easy to do if you are sitting down, and much laughter is caused.

The Tower of Pisa

Birds of a feather

A game much loved by little girls who delight in the art of persuasion. Half of the children go out of the room, and the other half sit round on the floor apart from each other and with a coloured napkin on the floor next to them. They all choose which child should be sitting next to them on coming into the room, and one by one the children enter and are begged by all the others to sit on a napkin next to those on the floor. If they choose the right person they stay in the room, but if they are wrong they retire outside again to a chorus of boos and hisses. When each child has chosen correctly, the teams change over and repeat the game.

Hunt the thimble

Hide the thimble in quite a difficult place, but so that it can be seen without moving objects. The children begin searching and on seeing the thimble sit down on the floor without saying a word. The whole search should be done in silence, although much giggling ensues, and the last person to see the thimble gets a booby prize. Try setting a time limit for older children.

Rhyme time

A nice quiet sitting-down game for everyone to get their breath back. Have a list of rhyming words prepared, such as 'tin', 'pin', 'fin', etc. and 'den', 'ten', 'when', etc. and start the game with 'I want a rhyme in jolly quick time, and the word I choose is HEN'. Each player then has to give a word that rhymes, but make sure you don't play this with too many children as it will get too difficult for them otherwise. It's ideal for a small party of four or five. Give everyone three chances, and if they fail three times to make a rhyme, they drop out.

Musical numbers

This is a good game for larger numbers of children in a big room. They all walk or skip round the room to music, and you act as the caller and operate the music. As soon as it stops you call out a number and the children have to get themselves into groups of that number as quickly as they can. So if you have twenty children and call out 'three' they will form themselves into groups of three. It follows that there will be two children over, so they are eliminated. With the new number of eighteen call out 'four' and there will be another two children out. The further apart they can be during the music the more exciting the game will be.

Animal pairs

A game for the older children who can read. Write names of well known animals onto cards and cut them in half, such as LI-ON, RAB-BIT, ELE-PHANT, GIR-AFFE, and divide the children into two teams. Pin the cards onto the children's backs so that pairs are in the same teams. The children then attempt to find their other half by asking

Animal pairs

questions such as 'What colour am I?', 'Have I stripes or spots?'. The first team to pair up correctly, wins. To make identifying the teams simple put a red or blue spot in the corner of each card.

Bean dropping

This has the merit of being deceptively simple and irritating to play! Have an empty jam jar for each child, and a bag of dried butter beans. Give ten to each child, then get them to stand in front of the jam jar with their legs straight, and drop the beans into the jar with their hands held at nose level. The first to finish successfully, wins.

Nose hockey

A team game that children love. Divide the party into the two teams, give each one a table tennis ball and stand them at one end of the room. Place two cushions well apart from each other on the floor at the other end of the room. At the start of 'go' the children have to take it in turns to 'nose' the ball up to the cushion, round it, and home again. On their hands and knees of course.

Grand change

Sit all the children in a largish circle and have one child in the middle blindfolded. The children are each named after the name of a well known town, and when you call the names of two of those towns, they have quietly to change places. The blindfolded child must try to catch somebody mid change over. If he succeeds, that person goes into the middle of the ring.

Yes and no

An amusing little game for a small party. One child sits in front of the others, and they take it in turns to ask him questions. If he answers 'yes' or 'no' in his reply he hands over to somebody else.

Hangman

Another game for a small group of children. Stand in front of them with a large sheet of paper pinned on a board. Think of a long word they will all know e.g. 'gingerbread', and put dashes for each letter on the paper (use felt tip pens or coloured pencils). Taking it in turns, they call out a letter, and if they choose correctly fill it in in the right place. If *not*, start drawing the hangman, a stroke for each incorrect letter, (see diagram). Anyone who guesses the correct word before you have completed the hangman is the winner.

Grandmother's footsteps

Grandmother's footsteps

The children stand in line with one child standing ahead of them with his back turned to them. At any given moment he can spin round, whereupon the rest of the children who are trying to creep up to him unawares, must stand stock still. If he sees anyone move they are out. If anyone reaches Grandmother they are the next Granny.

Wheelbarrow race

Arrange the children in pairs again. One child goes on its hands, and the other child holds its legs under his arms. The first pair to cross the finishing line wins.

Obstacle races

A great favourite with all children, the obstacles need not be very difficult as they are all arms and legs in their hurry, and find it difficult to master the simplest hurdle. Divide them into two teams – here are some suggestions for obstacles. Cardboard boxes with the bottom cut out to wriggle through. 'Rivers' of string parallel on the grass to jump over. Hats or adult wellington boots to put on and run in. Plastic ice cream containers half filled with water to be carried without spilling. Rugs to be wriggled under. Small hurdles to be jumped (put a stick across two bricks). Have about three obstacles for each child to complete before he finishes the race for the young ones, and increase them as they get older. Two adults will probably be needed to return things and sort things out whilst the next child is starting the course. For the smaller garden where there may not be much room, just get the children to do two hurdles and then turn round and come back again.

Out of doors

Five year olds will enjoy simple running races, but some are still very uncoordinated at this age so do not make the races too long. Here are some games that are always popular and do not require an enormous amount of athletic prowess.

Three legged race

Tie ankles together loosely for this game. Use something like a scarf or handkerchief. The first couple to finish the race, wins.

Three armed race

A variation on the three legged race for younger children. Tie their arms loosely together and get them to run to a finishing line.

Eight to ten years

This age group are in many ways the easiest to entertain. Confident of their skills, by the time the party is in full swing they will be eager for every game there is. By all means try games from the younger age group, the simplest ones can appeal to everyone, but older children often enjoy pitting their wits against each other with pencil and paper. Alternate rowdy games with peaceful games of concentration, and the time will fly by. There are some children, however, who are definitely *not* at their best with a pencil in their hands, and if one or two children show signs of sweeping the board in every game, keep these games to a minimum. A party is not school; children are there to enjoy themselves and not to feel stupid. Boys at this age need a lot of organisation, and a fine day in the garden for them is ideal.

Balloon bursting treasure hunt

A variation on the old treasure hunt, and excellent for boys. Write the clues on small pieces of paper and insert into the balloons before blowing them up. Number the clues – each clue leads to the next safety pin which is used to pop the next balloon – i.e. pin number 1 pops balloon number 1, which reveals clue number 2 which leads to pin number 2, etc. Children enjoy doing this in pairs; it's more fun to work the clues out together and easier to pop the balloons. Have a balloon at each stage for each pair, and the first couple to reach the last balloons gets the treasure.

Giant's necklace

Have about six cotton reels and a length of wool on two plates with a pair of rubber gloves beside them. Divide the children into two teams and get them to thread the cotton reels onto the wool wearing the rubber gloves. As soon as one child has completed a necklace it is dismantled, he runs back to his team and the next person attempts it. The first team to finish wins.

Reading in the train

Have a complete newspaper or comic for each child and muddle each paper up. Fold them neatly again, and hand one to each child. Sit them on the floor in a close circle. Now get them to sort their papers out; the first to do so is the winner.

Kim's game

Have about twenty objects on a tray and cover with a cloth. Bring the tray into the assembled children who have been given a pencil and paper each, and give them five minutes to look at the objects. Then remove the tray, and get them to list as many of the things as they can remember. Set a time limit and collect the papers in. The child with the most correct wins.

Kim's game

Roll the marble home

Cut a number of squares of different sizes out of the edge of one side of a cardboard box. Above each hole write a number; high numbers for the small holes, and low numbers for the larger ones. Divide the children into two teams. Place the box on the floor, stand the children behind a position in front of it, and get them in turn to roll six marbles each into the holes. The team or child with the highest score, wins.

Chocolate time

Several bars of chocolate, a knife and fork, and a plate are needed for this game. Sit the children in a circle and have the knife and fork and the chocolate on the plate in the middle. Each child throws a dice in turn and when they throw a six, rush into the middle and attempt to eat as much chocolate as they can by cutting it and eating it with the knife and fork. *No* hands allowed. They continue until the next person throws a six, when it is his turn. Added fun can be had by asking the child to put on a hat and scarf before attempting the task.

Chocolate time

Eye witness

Boys love this game. Explain that there has been a robbery, and a suspicious character was seen leaving the scene. Now take a volunteer outside the room, and help him dress up in an assortment of clothes, give him a bag to carry, a rolled newspaper, a stick or umbrella, anything that he wasn't wearing when he came to the party. Come into the room and tell the others that the suspect was seen running away and they have been asked to give an accurate description of him. As you shout 'Police' the child outside runs into the room, once round it, and out again, and the others have to write down anything he was wearing or carrying. The one with the most accurate list, wins. Then another child goes out, and dresses in another burglar's outfit.

Bat the balloon

Sit the children in two teams facing each other, preferably on chairs. Now toss a balloon between them, and the object of the game is to bat the balloon over the heads of the opposing team so that it falls to the ground behind them. No one is allowed to stand up: if they do, they drop out, so that team is a person short. No prizes, but great fun to play.

Lap against the clock

A hilarious game that teenagers enjoy too! All the children sit round in a circle with a dice and shaker. In the centre of the circle is a shallow bowl of orange juice and a bath hat. The children take it in turns to throw the dice and as soon as someone throws a six, that person runs to the middle, puts on the bath hat and laps the orange juice. As soon as the next six is thrown, that person takes over lapping the juice. No prizes here, just an amusing game for everyone.

Lap against the clock

Flour mountain

Flour mountain

Another game with no other intent than making the children laugh. Tightly pack a pudding basin with flour and invert on to a plate. On top of the flour put an unwrapped sweet. Stand the plate on some newspaper, put a spoon by it, and sit the children round in a circle. Each person then takes a spoonful from the flour mountain, and puts the flour in an empty bowl. One spoon each, and whoever lets the sweet fall has to put his hands behind his back and eat the sweet from the flour. It takes no time at all to rebuild the mountain.

Postman's holiday

An interesting game that children love. Clearly label a box with the name of a county such as Lancashire, and then underneath write the name of six towns in that county. Now label five more boxes, each with a different county and their towns in the same way, so you have thirty-six towns in all. (You can also do this with countries and capital cities for the younger age bracket.) Look in the index of a good road book to get ideas; try and confuse the issue by choosing several spellings such as Malden (Surrey) and Maldon (Essex). Now write all the names of the towns only on separate slips of paper, put them in a box, and put the six posting boxes around the house or garden. Have a pencil at hand and stand the children round the box. To start the game take a slip of paper out for each child, write their initials on it and hand it to them. At the given

signal they have to run off, post the town on the paper in the correct box and come running back for another slip. Be sure to mark each slip. The one with the most posted correctly, wins. Don't make the names *too* obscure!

Consequences

Very popular with children; they use the names of people they know and love the ridiculous situations that arise. Give each child a long piece of paper and a pencil. Start by asking them to write down the name of a man they know at the top of the paper then fold the paper over to conceal it, and pass it on. Next round is a woman they know, the next a place, then what he said to her, she said to him, and what the consequences were. Now a final pass round, and each child takes it in turn to open and read out his piece of paper.

Anagrams

A good game if you want to fill in some time and don't want a noisy game. Choose a subject such as flowers, zoo animals or towns, and write them clearly on a piece of card, but with the letters jumbled up i.e. LONDON becomes DOLONN. Don't make them too difficult, it's best to keep about three of the letters in their original order. Pin them up, give the children a pencil and paper each, and get them to write down as many correct solutions as they can in a set time.

Spinning the plate

Everyone sits in a wide circle on the floor, with one child in the middle. Give him an enamel plate, give each child in the circle a number, and tell them to remember it. The child in the middle then spins the plate and calls out a number as he does so. The child with that number has to dash to the centre and catch the plate before it falls to the ground. If he fails he drops out, if he catches it, he is the new plate spinner.

Charades

This needs little introduction, but for the uninitiated, divide the children into two groups and send one half out of the room. Those outside the door choose a word that can be divided into two halves and each half mimed as a separate word. The whole word is then mimed; three separate scenes in all. Some well-known words that divide are: dust-man, pen-cil, grand-father, lip-stick, sand-paper, car-pet. Act them as they sound, not as they are spelled, and if you have a dressing-up box so much the better. The team inside the room have to guess from the mimes what the word is. The game can be played by acting little scenes and bringing the words into the action, but this doesn't generally work with children; they find it difficult to introduce the spoken word spontaneously. Another variation is miming a well-known nursery rhyme, television programme, or book title.

Portrait drawing

Dumb Crambo

The party divides into two teams, and one side goes outside the door, whilst the half left in the room think of a word – say, 'light'. They summon in one person from outside, and tell them the word rhymes with – say, 'night'. This is relayed back and the team outside come in and all mime the word they think it is e.g. 'flight', by swooping up and down like birds. As this is incorrect, they are hissed, and retire outside the room to try again. They are clapped if the mime is correct, and the teams change over. The fun lies in trying to choose obscure words to baffle the other side. If a team is hissed incorrectly, the teams also change.

Tell me . . .

Prepare some cards with individual letters written boldly on them, and a list of questions such as 'A girl's name', 'the name of a bird', 'a colour', etc. Put the letter cards in a box, sit the children on the floor and have the questions by you. Ask the questions one by one, draw a letter out of the box and hold it up to show what the answer must begin with. The first person to shout out the most answers is the winner.

Portrait drawing

Have a large sheet of paper and some felt tip pens ready on a table. Blindfold each child in turn and lead them to the table saying: 'I want you to draw me a picture of . . . (naming a child at the party) can you do that for me?' The child picks up a felt tip pen with you saying, 'First draw me a face – thank you'. Tell them to pick up another pen and draw the eyes, nose, mouth etc., in turn until the face is completed, and the blindfold is taken off. Much laughter ensues as everyone watches the strange results.

Circle the stick

This is also seemingly very simple, but difficult to achieve. Boys in particular enjoy the challenge. Put a small bar of chocolate on the top of an up-turned jam jar on a table, and sit the children down about five yards from the table. Tell them they can eat the chocolate, but they must first stand up, put their foreheads on an umbrella handle with the point on the ground and turn round five times looking at the ground as they do so. Take the umbrella from them, and *now* see if they can get the chocolate.

77

Feel it

Inside the leg of a pair of thick tights put about ten to fifteen different objects such as a teaspoon, an apple, a small bottle, a walnut, a pencil, a folded handkerchief, a cotton wool ball, a squash ball, a mug – to name a few. Get the children in turns to feel them. Set a time limit for each child then ask them to write down as many objects as they could identify. The winner is the one who gets the most objects right.

Advertisements

Tear out from magazines or newspapers advertisements for well known products such as cereals or baked beans. Cut out any brand name that appears, number the pictures and stick them up. Give the children a time limit to identify as many brand names as they can.

Nursery rhymes

On a large sheet of paper copy out and number lines from various well-known nursery rhymes such as 'Little Jack Horner sat in a corner', 'The dish ran away with the spoon', 'And Jill came tumbling after', but leave out various key words such as: 'The — ran away with the —', 'Little — — sat in a —', and 'And — came tumbling —'. Ask the children to list the missing words. The one with the most correct, wins.

Musical islands

The children each take a partner, and a square of newspaper for each couple is put on the floor. They skip round the room hand in hand to music, and when the music stops they have to rush to an island, and stand on it. Next time the music stops the newspaper is folded once, and the pair has to fit on to it without falling off. Anyone who falls off is out. This may also be played singly by the children.

Heads and bodies

Another version of Consequences. Give all the children a long piece of paper and a pencil, and then ask them all to draw the head of a person. They then fold the paper over, and pass it on to the person next to them and they all draw a body. This is then folded over, passed on, and they all draw the legs. The paper is passed on for a final time, and everyone opens them up and looks at the results.

Draw it

A good game for the ten year olds. Divide the children into two teams, and each group chooses a leader. Both teams then decide on a book title, film or television programme, and write it on a piece of paper and fold it over. The leaders from each team then collect the piece of paper from the opposite side and at the word 'go', open the paper and without speaking, attempt to draw the title, so that his team can guess it. For instance,

'The Jungle Book' could be represented by a picture of a book, and lots of trees and creepers. The first team to guess correctly wins.

Missing adjectives

Not a competitive game, but very amusing for older children. Select a passage out of a book, or make up a little story, but write it down leaving a blank for the adjectives. The children then take it in turns to say an adjective each, and you write them into the story as they are said. They have no idea of the story of course, and when all the blanks are filled and the resulting story read back to them, it is often hilarious. An excellent game for adults too!

Passing the tissues

Divide the children into two teams again, sit them on the floor, and give each one a straw. Give the first child a tissue handkerchief square and tell them they have to pass it down the line by sucking it on the straw – no hands allowed unless the tissue is dropped, whereupon that child is allowed to pick it up and put it on the straw again. A game requiring quite a lot of concentration.

Smell it

Prepare a tray before the party with a number of different objects on it and place it away from everybody in another room. Choose things that have a distinctive smell such as instant coffee, peanuts, lemon juice, soap, antiseptic, a peppermint, an aniseed ball, an orange, and a drop of sherry in a glass. Then blindfold the children, bring them in one by one and get them to sniff each object in turn and tell you what it is. Not such a good game for a large party, as the children can get restless awaiting their turn.

Make a sentence

Have two large pieces of paper on a table with two felt tip pens beside them. Divide the children into two teams and put them at the other end of the room. To start the game call out any word that comes to your mind for instance 'go'; or 'when', 'where', etc. The first child dashes up and writes this on the paper and runs back. The next child then runs up and writes another word, any word, but it must follow on and make sense. The object is to have two turns each (or one if each team is a large one) and see which side makes the best sentence.

Balloon race

An old favourite, but everyone enjoys it. Line everybody up and give each child a balloon. At the word 'go' they have to put the balloon between their knees and run to the finishing line. If you have a large party you can divide them into two teams, and give each team a balloon. The children take it in turns to run to the finishing line and back again.

Pelmanism

There are some attractive sets of cards that you can buy to play this game, but playing cards do just as well. Sit all the children in a circle and deal all, or some of the cards, face down on the floor so that they are quite close to each other but not overlapping. The first child then turns over two cards at random; if they are a pair he keeps them, if not he turns them down again. The second child then has a turn, and after everyone has had a go, they have to begin to start remembering what all the cards are. Anybody who turns up a pair keeps it, and the child with the most pairs at the end wins.

Out of doors

Games for this age are more energetic and skilful and require a bit more organisation on your part. If your garden isn't large enough for the first two games, others will be more suitable, and remember, you can always have a there and back race.

Lurky

One child has a football by him, and closing his eyes counts to fifty whilst the rest hide. He then has to go and search for them, and must touch them before they reach the ball. Anyone who reaches it before he does, kicks it crying 'Lurky', and the game begins again with that child.

Slow bicycle race

Just as it says, so make sure the children are spaced well apart as there is a lot of wobbling. The *last* person to reach the finishing line is the winner. You will have to organise everyone to bring their own bicycles, but this game can be played in the local park or common, and at the same time a lot of other races can be organised round bicycles such as obstacle races.

Sack race

Hessian sacks nowadays are hard to find, but the strong paper ones that are used for dustbins are good substitutes. Hen food and flour also come in these, so if you know anyone with a supply of them, ask them to keep them for you. Put a child in a sack and line them up, and the first to jump over the finishing line is the winner.

Walking on bricks

Use any bricks for this game, but make sure they are all the same size. Two bricks per child, and they have to 'walk' on the bricks by putting one brick in front of them, balancing on it, moving the other brick in front, balancing on it, and so on. A very effective and amusing race.

Apple bobbing

Put a bucket of water on the grass and float some apples on it. Challenge the children to pick the apples up in their teeth, using no hands. This can

be turned into a team game by using two buckets of water, and getting the children to transfer an apple from the water to a basin with their teeth. This game is also suitable for younger children.

Going home

Pull the ball

Have two large rubber balls and two skipping ropes ready, and divide the children into two teams. Each child in turn has to pull a ball up the garden with the rope round the object and back again. Harder than it sounds, as it has to be done whilst walking backwards, so as to keep an eye on the ball.

This little piggy went to market

Divide the children into two teams and give each team a milk bottle and a strong stick. (Two walking sticks are ideal.) They have to put the bottle on its side, and push it up the course and back again with the stick. First to finish wins.

Go back home

Simple, but fun. The children are in two teams, and have to take it in turns to run backwards up the course and home again. The first team to finish wins.

Acknowledgments

The publishers would like to thank the following:
Campbell, Connelly & Co. Ltd: 66
John Cook: back of cover, 40, 42 (both), 44, 45, 46, 47 (both), 48, 50 (both), 51, 52, 53 (both), 54 (both), 55 (both)
By Mildred and Patty Hill © 1939 Summy Birchard Co. (USA). Reproduced by permission of Keith Prowse Publishing Co. Ltd, 138–140 Charing Cross Rd, London WC2H OLD: 41
Dr A. A. G. Lewis: 31
Sandra Lousada: front cover, half-title, title page, 4, 6, 8, 9, 11 (both), 12, 13, 14, 15, 16, 25, 26, 28, 30 (both), 32 (both), 33, 35, 36, 37, 56, 58, 59 (both), 60, 62, 63, 68, 69 (both), 70, 71 (both), 72, 73, 74, 75 (both), 77, 78, 79
London Transport: 35
By courtesy of McDonald's Golden Arches Restaurants Ltd: 37
Party Place The Party Shop, 67 Gloucester Ave, London NW1 8LD Tel: 01-586 0169: 10 (for hire of mould) and supplying various props in the food photographs. A General Catalogue can be supplied on sending a stamped addressed envelope. Special catalogues available for: Christmas, Easter and Halloween. Closed on Mondays and throughout August.
The Science Museum, London: 38 (both)
Upstream Theatre Club, St Andrew's, Short Street, Waterloo, London SE1 8LJ Tel: 01-928 5394: 36
The Zoological Society of London: half-title, 32 (below), 33 (Birthday lunches can be arranged at London Zoo throughout the year. These include a special birthday cake. Full details are available from the Catering Manager)

Index